THE
Archive Photographs
SERIES

ISLEWORTH

Francis H. N. Glossop and his wife, Ann Fish Glossop, c.1860. Ann (1824-87) was the daughter of Henry Pownall of Spring Grove House. Francis (1815-86) was Chairman of the Brentford Magistrates, Treasurer of the Isleworth Feoffee and Almshouse Trusts, Chairman of Feltham Industrial Schools, and a Deputy Lieutenant of Middlesex. He was the eldest son of Revd H. Glossop, Vicar of All Saints', and lived at Silverhall, North Street.

THE
Archive Photographs
SERIES

ISLEWORTH

Compiled by
Mary and Kevin Brown

CHALFORD

First published 1995
Copyright © Mary and Kevin Brown, 1995

The Chalford Publishing Company
St Mary's Mill, Chalford,
Stroud, Gloucestershire, GL6 8NX

ISBN 0 7524 0346 X

Typesetting and origination by
The Chalford Publishing Company
Printed in Great Britain by
Redwood Books, Trowbridge

*This book is dedicated to the memory of George Brown,
for his support and encouragement over many years.*

Isleworth Brewery, St John's Road, c.1910. The Brewery is now demolished and lorries long ago replaced the horse transport. Now, the past importance of the working horse is remembered by the street names: Drayman's way, Percheron Close, Clydesdale Close, Shire Horse Way, and the Brewery Mews Business Centre – all built on the former Brewery site.

Contents

Dumb Bell Drill, Spring Grove High School, 1908. Although we do not know the exact location of this school it flourished until c.1919, when an advertisement read: 'Spring Grove High School for Girls, Osterley, with Preparatory School for Boys, and Kindergarten. Sound general education on modern lines. Pupils prepared most successfully for all examinations. Special classes for secretarial work. Individual attention. Gymnasium, games. Very moderate fees. Sanitation perfect.'

Acknowledgements

The majority of the illustrations in this book are taken from the authors' collection, and we would like to thank all those who, over the years, have allowed us to borrow photographs to copy or who have shared their memories of Isleworth with us.

In particular we would like to thank the following people who have provided illustrations or information used in this book:

Mrs N. Anderson, Mr Paul Andrews (Licensee, Red Lion public house), Miss Doreen Ayres, Mrs Gilda Bagnall, Mrs Olive Beech, the late Mrs H. Bidgood, Mrs Olive Breden, Mr Ken Cooper, Mrs T. Caudell, Mr Doug Cotterell, Miss Grace Cousins, Mr Steve Davison (Licensee, The Castle public house), Mr Peter Downes, Fr C. Dychoff, Miss Marion Easton, the late Mr Stanley Evans, Mr Bruce Fenn, Mrs Ena Field, Mrs Jennie Fisher, Mr Harry Florey, Miss Doris Francis, Mr and Mrs Harry Goddard, Mrs Joan Hailstone, Mrs Maureen Harris, the late Mr Wally Harverson, Mrs M. Hill, Mrs Janet Ion, Mrs Jean Lagden, Mrs Joyce Lane, Mrs M. Lang, Mrs J. Lingwood, the late Mrs V. McCoy, the late Mr Ernie Manning, Mr John Middleton, Mrs I. Morris, the staff of Nazareth House, Miss N. Newton, Miss Joan Over, the late Mr A. Payne, Mr and Mrs A. Peacock, Mrs D. Pearce, Mrs D. Quinn, Mrs E. Robertson, Mrs M. Sharman, Mrs Eileen Sheridan, Mrs Theresa Turner, the late Mr Pat Voller, Miss Norah Weathers, Miss A. Wells,Mr Tommy White, the late Mrs Eva Willshire, and the late Mr Edward Young.

We should also like to thank the staff of the local studies department in Hounslow Library for their assistance while we were researching this book.

Introduction

There has probably been a settlement at Isleworth for about 4,000 years, although the earliest written record dates from AD 695, when the name is recorded as Gislheresuuyrth. It would be impossible to give a detailed history of any village covering this period in one book, especially in a book of photographs. Many buildings (and people) important in Isleworth's history disappeared long before the invention of photography – buildings including the old moated Manor House, Kendall House, Shrewsbury House, the first Silver Hall, and the Callico Mills. Similarly for others, no suitable photographs were available to us – Mandeville House, Heddon House, the Coach and Horses on the Richmond Road, and the Isleworth Fair, formerly held in the streets around Lower Square, come to mind. Within these limitations, however, we have tried to make this book as comprehensive as possible.

The late nineteenth and early twentieth centuries have seen a rapid and far-reaching series of changes in everyday life. The introduction of electric lighting, of the wireless and television, the advent of the telephone, car, aeroplane and the computer have all affected our daily lives. Changes in medical science have altered life expectancy and two World Wars have changed the old social order for ever. These changes have been paralleled locally as Isleworth has gradually changed from a village into a suburb. Local government has changed from Parish to Urban District to London Borough – each more remote from the people they serve. The vast areas of market gardens formerly supplying the needs of London's population have been replaced by housing. Employment opportunities have changed with the loss of Kidds Mill, Isleworth Brewery, Pears Soap Factory, and the river industries. With these changes has come an enormous increase in population and a consequential increase in services – new shops, schools and churches, etc. Despite these changes and the recent redevelopment of some of the older parts of Isleworth, there still remains something of a village atmosphere.

It is fortunate that this period of change coincided with the development of photography. While private camera ownership was not so common at the beginning of this century as it is now, local photographers produced thousands of images, often in the form of picture postcards, recording local events, people, and buildings. Where these photographs have survived they provide an important, and sometimes unique, record of the times. Detailed reporting in the local papers of the day is often helpful in completing a 'picture' of local history, providing a written account to complement the old photographs.

National history may be seen in the lives of politicians, prelates and kings. Local history is similarly mirrored in the lives of local people – shopkeepers, publicans, market gardeners and tradesmen, teachers and schoolchildren: the 'ordinary' people so often omitted in more 'official' histories which chronicle great houses, estates, churches, and civic bodies. We have been very privileged to be able to share the memories and photographs of some old Isleworth residents, for their family histories are part of local history, and unfortunately all too often go unrecorded.

Isleworth will mean different things to different people – the church by the river with its ancient tower and plague pit; the wharves with their cranes; the old Ferry and the Ait covered in osiers; the many inns and almshouses, or shopping in narrow, winding South Street; for older residents, pleasant memories of less hurried days, of schooldays and blossom-filled fruit orchards; for the younger generation these images will be a glimpse of a vanished way of life. We hope there will be something in this book to interest everyone.

All Saints' Church, Church Street, 1938. The nave and galleries were built in 1706, to a modified design by Sir Christopher Wren, and the chancel was added in 1866-7, largely financed by the Farnell family. Mr William Farnell presented the East Window, which featured scenes of the Passion. Below the south gallery can be seen the War Memorial Chapel, added in 1919. The church was destroyed by arson in 1943.

One

Isleworth
The Old Village

The medieval village of Isleworth on the bank of the Thames had twin centres in the church and the Manor House. In 1415 the Manor was part of Henry V's endowment of the new Syon Monastery that following the dissolution became Syon House, the seat of the Dukes of Northumberland. Gradually the focus of the village changed as South Street became the main thoroughfare with employment provided by the many trades associated with the river, in the Mills, and in agriculture on the surrounding land.

All Saints' Church, c.1910. The tower (late fourteenth century) is the oldest part of the church, with a nave rebuilt in 1706 and a chancel added in 1866-7. The building was largely destroyed by arson in 1943 and a new church, incorporating the surviving old tower, opened in 1970.

War Memorial Chapel, Isleworth

All Saints' War Memorial Chapel, 1920, dedicated to St Michael and St George, was erected in the South Aisle at a cost of £1,000 and constructed from plans by Mr W.S. Weatherly. It included a roll of honour on an oak tablet to the 176 Isleworth men who died in the First World War. The inscription at the base read 'His life for his country – His soul to God'. The chapel was dedicated on 14 December 1919 by the Bishop of London, and the oak tablet was dedicated on 6 November 1920. Sadly, it was destroyed in the 1943 fire and the record of names is lost.

Mary Hicks, August 1870, aged 104. Mary Hicks was born at Brosley, Shropshire, on 11 August 1766. She was one of many young women from that area who walked to Isleworth to find work in the local market gardens and in carrying garden produce to market in London. Mary married a local man, John Hicks, and died on 24 November 1870 aged 104, having spent the last 27 years of her life as an inmate of Brentford Union Workhouse. Her tombstone in All Saints' churchyard was erected 'By private subscription of the Guardians'.

Sale of Work 25 June 1919. The Duchess of Northumberland performing the opening ceremony at a Sale of Work to raise funds for the War Memorial Chapel in All Saints' Church. A guard of honour is provided by 30 members of All Saints' (1st Isleworth) Guides under Captain Bradley. The sale was held in the Vicarage garden (41 Church Street). The Vicar, Revd M. Relton is seated in the centre of the picture.

1st Isleworth (All Saints') Girl Guide Company, c.1915. Members of the Daffodil Patrol, including, from left to right: first; Kathleen Harrington, second; Winnie Smith, fourth; Muriel Tebbutt and seventh; Doris Balando, in costume for a concert. During the First World War, members of the Company, led by Captain Moyes and Lieutenant Bradley, helped with sewing at Percy House Military Hospital.

Syon House, c.1930. The house was built c.1550 and is now the seat of the Duke of Northumberland. Syon occupies the site of the former Bridgettine Monastery founded by Henry V in 1415 and dissolved by Henry VIII in 1539. The interior of the house was redesigned by Robert Adam in the 1760s and the grounds laid out by Capability Brown.

Cattle at Syon Park, 1903. In recent years the estate surrounding Syon House has altered greatly. The former private gardens are now open to the public with a large garden centre adjoining. The parkland, where cattle and pigs were kept, is now a venue for public events and contains a trout fishery, butterfly house, aquatic centre, and car park for visitors to these and the other attractions on the estate.

Red Cross Hospital, Syon, 1915, with nursing staff outside the stables at Syon, now part of the garden centre. In 1914 the riding school opened as a Red Cross hospital with the Duchess of Northumberland as Commandant, Dr Bolt as Principal Medical Officer, and Mrs Peinge as Matron. In May 1916 Blue School Infants visited the wounded, taking as gifts 86 oranges, 69 new laid eggs, 294 cigarettes, 5 apples, one box of chocolates, 14 bananas, 10 bunches of flowers, one pot of fish paste, one box of matches, 10 buns, and one box of cigarette papers.

London Road, c.1905. The Lion Gateway was designed by Robert Adam in 1773 for the first Duke of Northumberland as a grand entrance to the Syon House estate. To the right can be seen the eighteenth-century Coach and Horses public house, mentioned by Charles Dickens in *Oliver Twist* and having a first floor bow window like so many inns on this once important coaching road.

Coach and Horses, London Road, 1907. Although no longer a coaching inn, the proprietor, then Mr James Harris, continued to meet the needs of travellers. Advertised were 'Good stabling' and 'accommodation for motors and cycles' and 'bed and breakfast from 3/-'.

George Manville Fenn, 1831-1909, born in Pimlico and educated privately before briefly becoming a teacher. Fenn quickly became a prolific journalist and author, writing over 100 adventure stories for boys including 'Brownsmith's Boy', set in the market gardens of Isleworth. From 1889-1909 Fenn lived at Syon Lodge on the London Road, designed in 1780 by the Adam Brothers as the Dower House to Syon House. The nearby sheltered accommodation, Fenn House, is named after him. Fenn is buried in the Park Road cemetery.

Isleworth Cemetery, Park Road, 1912. The Cemetery opened in 1880. Many of the trees there were planted by Mr John Weathers of Silverhall Nursery in 1902. The large monument, centre right, commemorates Andrew Pears of Pears Soap fame, who died on 10 January 1909 aged 63, and also his son Thomas, who was lost on the SS *Titanic*.

Father Eric Green, 1870-1929. Following ordination in 1896 Fr Green held several posts, including that of parish priest of the Cathedral Parish at the newly-opened Westminster Cathedral. In 1906 he was appointed Rector of Isleworth. Here he initiated the building of St Bridget's Church, the Church Hall, Presbytery and St Mary's School, and revived processions honouring the Catholic Martyrs of Isleworth. He volunteered in 1914, served as chaplain in Gallipoli and France, and was awarded a Military Cross for distinguished service. Returning to Isleworth he helped form the local branch of the British Legion, serving as Vice-President, and supported moves to build the local War Memorial. He died in 1929 having served 23 years in Isleworth, and is buried in Park Road Cemetery. He was a much-loved man, and thousands of local people lined the streets for his funeral, which was attended by many civic and church dignitaries, including Cardinal Bourne, Archbishop of Westminster.

Catholic Martyrs Procession, Park Road, c.1927. Left, Fr Eric Green, Parish Priest from 1906 to 1929; second left, Joseph Weathers (?), County Councillor; and second right, Patrick Murphy, JP, manager of the Flour Mills, who, in 1932, presented the mace to the new Borough of Heston and Isleworth. The Annual Martyrs Procession honoured Richard Reynolds, Confessor of Syon Monastery and John Hale, Vicar of Isleworth, who were executed in 1535 for refusing to acknowledge Henry VIII's supremacy over the Church. Ferry House can be seen in the background.

Ferry House staff, c.1910. Built in the seventeenth century and re-fronted in the eighteenth century, Ferry House was badly damaged by incendiary bombs in 1942, but has since been restored. When this photograph was taken the owner was Mr Powis Lomas, JP, Secretary and Comptroller of the Great Eastern Railway Co. He was a trustee of Isleworth Charities, a School Governor, and Churchwarden at All Saints'. An earlier resident in the house was the artist J.M.W. Turner.

Isleworth Church Ferry, 1924. Church Ferry, or Isleworth Ferry, began during the reign of Henry VIII. It was for pedestrians only. It was closed in 1939, re-opening during summer weekends after the war, but it ceased completely c.1963. Ferry men included Samuel Styles, Thomas Finn, Charlie Simmons (40 years' service), Harry Sims, 'Titch' Simmonds, and Cornelius Dargon (approx. 40 years' service). The ancient ferry rights, which had lain unused for nearly two decades, were acquired by Speyhawk, who made them available to three local residents, and in July 1983 river enthusiasts Adam Cade, the actor Simon Rouse, and Chris Maciejowski took it in turns to ferry passengers across the river. Public support of this venture was not very good and so the service lapsed. The rights of the ferry have since been purchased by Jonathan Radgick, who teamed up with local boatbuilder R.J. Woods, and operations re-commenced on 8 July 1995 between Isleworth Church on the Middlesex bank and the Old Deer Park on the Surrey bank.

Ferry, All Saints Isleworth.

River front, 1903. On the left is the London Apprentice and on the right, All Saints' Church. On the foreshore the Ferryman works on his boat while cargo is being unloaded from a sailing barge onto horse-drawn carts. In the centre can be seen the end wall of Porch House, built c.1706 using stone from the medieval church and demolished in 1902. Butter Field House now occupies this site.

River Front, 1909. The Thames has always been important to Isleworth as a highway, trade route, and leisure facility. A great variety of vessels have used the river, from the dug-out canoes of the earliest inhabitants to modern power boats. Here, a Thames sailing barge, rowing boat, skiff and sailing boat are using the river at the same time, but cross-channel cargo boats, canal boats, paddle steamers, and royal state barges have all used the river here.

Tolson's Almshouses, Church Street, c.1950. These almshouses were founded in 1750 as the gift of Mrs Ann Tolson to house six widows or spinsters and six bachelors. By 1860 the almshouses had become decrepit and new buildings (shown here) were erected on an adjacent site given by John Farnell and entered through an elaborate archway with the men and women housed on opposite sides of the courtyard. In 1959, these buildings were sold and replaced by Tolson House in North Street.

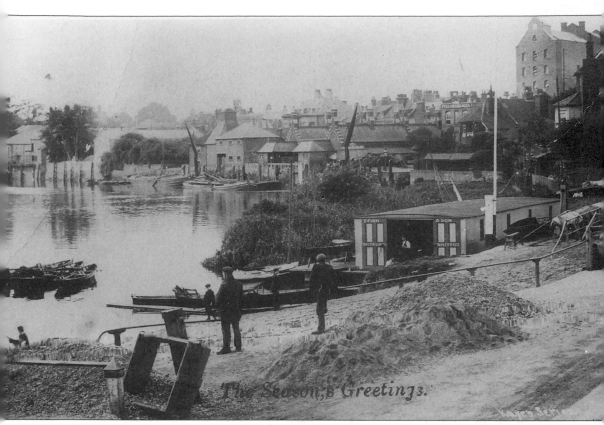

The Season's Greetings.

River Front, 1904. In the foreground are heaps of gravel and sand unloaded from barges and awaiting collection. The bottomless box was used to measure a yard of sand. At centre right, sheltered by the small islet, is E. Finn's boathouse where rowing boats could be hired and repaired. The boathouse, affectionately known as the 'ark', floated on pontoons and served as the headquarters of the Isleworth Rowing Club, whose pennant would be flown from the flagpole. In the background, extreme right, is the corner of the London Apprentice with Isleworth Mill Buildings behind, dominating the scene. To the left of the Mill, the sign 'Fullers Ales' can be seen on the rear of the Orange Tree public house. Further left can be seen the distinctive stepped roofs of Tolson's Almshouses and behind them the tall building with two prominent chimneys and two bay windows is Holland House, a fine eighteenth-century building that was once the home of Mr Henry Farnell. Further left the steep-roofed building was once used as a malthouse, and immediately behind this can be seen the turret on top of the Old Blue School. Mooring posts line this stretch of the river, some with Thames sailing barges moored up. As always, the river scene has attracted a number of onlookers.

Isleworth Rowing Club Ladies' Senior Four, c.1935, the champion rowers from 1931 to 1938 who represented England in international events. They are shown together with some of the trophies they had won. Left to right: Stroke, Phyll Taylor; No. 2, Kate Davis (later Young); Cox, 'Did' Gould; Bow, Amy Tompkins; and No. 3, Grace Chapman (later Phipps).

Members of Isleworth Rowing Club, c.1925, photographed in the grounds of All Saints' Vicarage (then 41 Church Street), wearing Club colours and showing some of the trophies awarded at the Club regatta. The Club was formed in 1924 with a nucleus of eight men. By 1932, in the Club's heyday, there were 100 male and 30 female members. A ladies' section had been added in 1925. The club headquarters was a floating boathouse known as 'The Ark' that was moored on the foreshore about 20 yards from the London Apprentice. The club ceased to exist in the early 1940s.

All Saints' Church, and the wedding of Kate Davis and Edward Young is taking place, 6 February 1938. Both were members of Isleworth Rowing Club and Club members provided a Guard of Honour with crossed oars. Note the Club Colours on the oar blades. Edward and his brother helped their father in the well-known upholstery business at Richmond. Kate had a sweet shop in South Street, and later a hairdressing business.

River Front, 1909. Barges await the tide and the ferryman awaits passengers. This stretch of the foreshore has long been a free-draw dock.

'Port of Isleworth', c.1905. A familiar sight at Isleworth, here the *James* shows how well the flat-bottomed Thames barges 'took to the ground' at low tide. To the right stands All Saints' Church, and behind the barge, with the bow window, the London Apprentice. The low islet has recently washed away but children still cannot resist paddling here.

The view from the Old Blue School roof, c.1926. This unique view was photographed by Mr T. White when he was repairing the school clock. Across the rooftops to the left can be seen All Saints' Church and, in the centre, Isleworth Ait, then used to grow osiers, which were woven into baskets for local market gardens. The Ait is now a nature reserve.

The view from All Saints' tower, c.1962. In the foreground are the London Apprentice and Church Street roofs, to the centre are cranes at Bridge Wharf, and in the distance Lion Wharf is busily unloading cargo. Between the cranes, near the horizon, is Nazareth House – once a children's home but now a retirement home. Below the tall chimney can be seen the flats in Magdala Road, with Holland House immediately in front of them. On the extreme right, in the background, is the new Blue School.

Church Street, 8 April 1939; on the left is the London Apprentice, in the centre the Church Street Houses are mainly Georgian although the two cottages nearest the church were built c.1904 on the site of Porch House. In 1969 these were re-fronted and converted into one building, Butter Field House.

Lion Wharf at low tide, *c*.1930. Cranes are busily unloading cargo from the ships, which carried a cross-Channel trade until the 1960s. Now totally redeveloped, the name Lion Wharf Road reflects a lost trade.

The London Apprentice, Church Street, *c*.1900. A large bay window was added to the first floor in 1906, but the exterior of the building is largely unaltered. The lady by the doorway may be Miss Kemp, who was proprietress at the turn of the century. Several of the children have hoops – no video games for them!

Church Street, *c*.1950. Many large loads have come up the Thames to the Draw Docks at Isleworth. Here, a barge has been loaded onto a lorry for road transport, although barely able to pass through the narrow street. First floor balconies here have often been damaged by such wide loads. No width restriction in Church Street then!

Church street flooding in the 1950s, a regular occurrence before the erection of flood defences in 1979. There are plaques set in the wall outside All Saints' Church recording some notable floods. The site behind the tall wall is now Millside Place, and from the place where the people are standing an alley now runs to Snowy Fielder Waye.

Church Street, c.1905, seen from the Mill Bridge with Mill Plat to the left. The two groups of cottages were demolished early this century. The site was later used as a transport yard and for warehousing, but has now been redeveloped as a housing complex called Millside Place.

Samuel Kidd's Mill, c.1910. There have been water-powered flour mills in Isleworth since 1066, originally situated by the River Crane, but following the cutting of the Duke's river in the 1530s near Church Street. Kidd's Mill, the latest and last of these mills, was a major local employer. It closed in 1934 and the buildings were demolished in 1941. On the left is the Mill Bridge in Church Street, and to the right the cottages on the corner of Mill Plat where Millside Place now stands.

Mill Basin, c.1913. Barges entered the Mill Basin from the Thames by lowering their sails and masts and passing under the Church Street Bridge. Once in the Mill Basin they moored alongside the Mill beneath the three overhanging lucams to unload grain and load sacks of flour. Note the hanging sailcloth canopy, which could be drawn to allow work to continue in bad weather, and the curved planks to cover the barge's cargo.

Kidd's Mill 'Sentinel' lorry, c.1925. Kidd's Mill was very progressive and one of the most modern in the London area. In 1894 the building was converted from stone-mill to roller-mill. Transport too was modernised very early. Here, the first of a fleet of steam-driven Sentinel lorries is seen. This was driven by Mr Alfred Pike.

Mill Plat, 1918, mill workers near the entrance to Warkworth House. In 1918 mill girls worked from 6.00am to 6.00pm, receiving 10/- per week. Work was hard, including carrying heavy sacks of grain, and the hygiene was strict, the workers wearing overalls and caps. Once a year the whole mill was closed to be fumigated.

Ingram's Almshouses, Mill Plat, 1973, endowed in 1664 by Sir Thomas Ingram. Sir Thomas, who lived in Isleworth, was Chancellor of the Duchy of Lancaster, and is buried in Westminster Abbey. These six almshouses have recently been extensively renovated and modernized.

North Street, c.1920, facing the Twickenham Road. Behind the wall Silver Hall can be seen, which was built in 1850 for Revd Henry Glossop. From 1899 to 1908 it was used as a convent by Carmelite nuns, and subsequently as a girls' boarding school, Collingwood College. The house was demolished c.1950, the grounds becoming a public park, Silverhall Gardens, in the 1960s.

Collingwood College, Isleworth. The Girl Guides.

Collingwood College Girl Guides, c.1924. Collingwood College was a short-lived private boarding school (c.1917-1936), occupying Silver Hall. The guide company was formed in November 1922 and disbanded in 1926. During this time the officers included Miss R. Dowling of Chiswick, Miss L.W. Elphrick of Collingwood College, and Miss G. Ashbee of Ealing.

Outside 18 Percy Gardens, 1913. Mrs Eleanor Manning (*née* Beadle) with children Alice and Henry. Percy Gardens extended between North Street, opposite the Methodist Chapel, and the Duke's River, with terraced houses on both sides. Residents were responsible for maintaining and shoring up the banks of the Duke's River where it bordered Percy Gardens. In 1961 the terraces were compulsorily purchased by the Council, demolished, and new flats, also called Percy Gardens, were erected on the site.

W.T. Manning and E.J. Manning, c.1910. Before the coming of the motor car, cycling was a popular pastime for many, allowing the working classes to get out into the countryside, and promoting good health. Many cycling clubs were formed with time trials and road races being common events. Here, William Thomas Manning and his son Ernest John Manning, both born in Isleworth, prepare for an outing on their tandem, said to be a 'chater leigh' machine.

British Legion members ready for an outing in 1929. For many years the headquarters of the Isleworth branch (founded in 1927) was the former Methodist Chapel, Wesley Hall, in North Street, pictured here. Wesley Hall was bult in 1835 with box pews, a high pulpit, and a west gallery with pipe organ. A Sunday School room was added in 1839. The chapel closed early this century. The building was demolished when North Street was redeveloped and the Legion moved to the present purpose-built clubhouse.

C. Mayger's letterhead, 1909. The family firm of Maygers have been undertakers in Isleworth since the 1850s, occupying Alma House, 26 North Street (demolished in 1960 – the new Blue School occupies the site). Charles Mayger was succeeded by his sons Charles and Frederick. Charles Jnr was apprenticed to his father in 1897 and did not retire until 1960, when the firm closed. When the firm bought a motorised hearse the old glass carriage found use an an aviary for budgerigars!

North Street from Swan Street, *c.*1905, on the right the building beyond the advertising hoardings and the one with the 'S bar' stand either side of Downton Place, which ran between North Street and the Northumberland Arms. The entrance to the present Blue School occupies the site of the terrace on the left, and the houses and shops opposite have been replaced by The Green and the buildings of Manor House Way.

Lower Square, *c.*1905. Two buildings have long dominated Lower Square, on the right the old Blue School and on the left the Northumberland Arms, built in 1834 for Mr H. Limpus, now converted to offices and renamed Waverley House. Left of the Blue School is the sign 'Eastwood and Co. – Lime, cement and brick merchants', and in the distance can be seen cottages in Church Street.

Northumberland Arms Cork Club, 1920, the members posing with a horse-drawn break outside the Inn prior to an outing to Maidenhead. Each member had to carry a cork and was fined 6d. if unable to produce one. Standing, left to right: -?-, Beach Shortland, Annie Sanderson, Nell Gaul, -?-, Mrs Scarlet, -?-, -?-, -?-, Mrs McElwan, Mrs Jones. On brake: Ivy Bowen, Kate Savory, Jane Armitage, Mrs Evans, Polly Taylor, Mrs Thomas, Mrs York, -?-, Mrs York, and Mrs Shortland.

Church Street, 1913, seen from Lower Square looking towards Mill Basin with Kidd's Mill in the centre dominating the scene.

Blue School boys' gymanstic drill, 1904. No special equipment and no uniform and no PE kit, although some of the boys have changed into soft shoes leaving a line of boots by the wall.

Eight Little Mothers

'Eight little mothers', 1915. Blue School pupils dressing up, with dolls as babies. Perhaps this picture was based on a popular song of the period performed at a school concert. Back row, left to right: -?-, Mary Spriggs, -?-. Middle row: 'Dolly Sisman, -?-, Grace Hoad. Front row: ? Bowen and 'Gerty' Hatt. Grace Hoad was six years old when this photograph was taken.

Blue School girls' Empire Day display, c.1910. Inaugurated in 1902 to commemorate Queen Victoria's birthday (24 May), Empire Day was celebrated with patriotic pride in schools throughout the country. With Britannia in the centre and the Union Jack, these girls are wearing sashes proclaiming Liberty, Mercy, Patience, Justice, Faith, and Victory.

Blue School pupils crowning the May Queen, c.1920. Traditional festivities were still celebrated in local schools in the 1920s. This photograph shows the crowning of the Blue School May Queen and the celebration would have included a dance around the maypole, which can be seen centre back of the group photograph.

Blue School, Lower Square, c.1925. The history of the Blue School can be traced back to 1630. This building was built as a school in 1841 and used as such until 1939. It has had several uses since then. The buildings to the right, in Swan Street, including the early-seventeenth-century cottages with the high chimneys, were demolished in 1953.

Swan Street, 1920, part of the Remembrance Day procession. The parade included a band, ex-servicemen, police, nurses, schoolchildren, scouts, guides, etc. On the right can be seen the Swan public House. First recorded in 1722, this building was rebuilt in the 1930s. Next door is the Swan Haircutting and Shaving Salon with the barber's pole outside.

Upper Square, c.1905. On the left is J. Lee's greengrocer's shop; on the right, awnings show May Blossom Restaurant and E. Roe's shop; next is The Swan, and beyond, houses in North Street which were demolished c. 1960. Swan Street lies hidden behind the public house. The drinking fountain was erected in 1870 as a memorial to Revd Henry Glossop, the vicar of All Saints' from 1821-1854.

Upper Square, c.1900. Left to right: Edward Roe, Wine and Spirit Merchant; the May Blossom Restaurant; Charles Riminton, newsagent; J. Killin, watchmaker; and on the corner, Barclays Bank. Barclays eventually incorporated both Killin and Riminton's shops before closing in 1993. Note the penny farthing (on the left) hanging above the Isleworth Cycle Stores at 2 South Street. Many Isleworth children learned to ride on machines hired from Mr Hill, who ran the shop.

Upper Square, c.1903. In the centre is the Castle Inn; to its left, part of Gavin's Tobacconist; and on the right, with the white tiles, Carter's Butchers, then Witchers Groceres. On the extreme left is part of The Swan; then, with the bow window, Edward Roes, a Wine/Spirit Merchant and Grocer who also ran a Post Office, hence the wall-mounted pillar box. The bow window was removed in the 1930s when the shop was remodelled.

Castle Inn, 18 Upper Square, 1914. The landlord, Samuel Vine, is standing in the doorway. A trapdoor leads directly from the pavement to the cellar. This building was demolished and replaced with a new one before 1930. The 'Entire' advertised would have been 'porter or stout as delivered from the Brewery'. Serving, like most local inns, as a community centre, the Castle was once headquarters of the Ancient Order of Oddfellows. It also had a loan society based there. In 1815, the rateable value was £15.

Group outing from The Castle, 1946. Among those gathered outside the new Castle Inn for an outing are, left to right: 1. Jim Davis, 2. Mick Field, 5. Jim Kennedy, 6. Ernie Manning, 7. Harold Winterbottom, 9. Jim Davis Jnr, 10. Con Dargon (Isleworth Ferryman), 13. George Monk, 17. Don Gilroy (landlord of The Castle), 22. Ted Collier, 25. George Epthite Jnr, 26. John Gernerkelic (Royal Netherlands Navy), and 29. George Epthite.

Nazareth House, 1992, built for Sir William Cooper in 1833 on the site of an earlier building and originally called Isleworth House. In 1892 the house was bought by an Order of Catholic Nuns and the name changed to Nazareth House. New buildings have been erected in the grounds, including a chapel consecrated in 1902. In addition to the conventual use, the complex provided a children's home, now closed, and more recently, accommodation for elderly people.

South Street from Upper Square, 1905. On the right is Hermann Sahler's renowned bakery at 1 Upper Square; next door is Isleworth Cycle Stores; next, a confectioner's, followed by the Village Dairy run by George Connell, which also sold corn and other provisions. Opposite, the light-fronted shops were Thomas Stacey, baker and Warple Bros, boot makers. These shops later became a pawnbroker's. Next door stands the Royal Standard, the signboard showing against the sky.

South Street, c.1915. Compare this with the previous picture: the Royal Standard has closed and the shops next door have been rebuilt. Electric lighting has replaced the gas lamps, but the street is still narrow and winding. On the right, billboards show where the Public Hall lies back from the street. Beside Church House (with the bay window) an alley leads to the Mission Church and Church Hall. The buildings on the left have now been demolished and Shrewsbury Walk occupies the site.

Old Isleworth Musical Society Concert, 20 January 1936, held in the Church Hall, South Street, to celebrate the golden wedding of Mr and Mrs A.T. Hare of the 'Orangery', St Margaret's Drive, St Margaret's. The programme included a performance of Mr Hare's cantata *Ode to Joy*. All Saints' Church Hall and the adjacent Mission Church stood behind the South Street shops, near the Public Hall, with access through an alley. Both buildings have been demolished and the Blue School new hall, opened in 1986, occupies the site.

South Street, 1914, facing Upper Square, right, and level with the top of the bus, jars show Leach Brothers, Oil and Colour Men. Next door, Stanley Nixon was an agent for Pier House Laundry, and a photographer – he took this picture. Then comes Frederick Hutton, fishmonger; John Taylor, bootmaker; John Beal, butcher; Albert Wenden, hairdresser – note the bottles in the window; and with the handcart outside, Mrs Minnie Cow, furniture dealer. This parade was demolished and Shrewsbury Walk erected on the site c.1960.

South Street, 1914, facing Upper Square. From left, Frederick Helsdon, tobacconist; Abraham Byford, hairdresser – 'Gents Haircut 3d, Shaving 1d, Boys Haircut 2d'; Dr Bulger's surgery; and with the white tiles, John Cox, butchers. The advertising hoardings show where the public hall lies back from the street. On the right, showing against the rooftops of Upper Square, is the signboard of the Royal Standard. Worple Road turns off far right by the shed marked 'Printing Works', which stood in front of the King's Arms and had short-term occupants.

Charles Pile, Farriers, 1911. Built at the corner of South Street and Worple Road in 1887 for George Deane, and later run by Charles Pile, who in 1911 advertised as a 'Wheelwright, Spring and Tyre Smith, General Smith's and Shoeing Forge'. The forge was converted into a motor repair garage in the 1930s, when cars and lorries began to replace horses, and is still used as a garage today – Jubilee Works.

South Street, February 1929 – children racing for soup. Severe cold weather in February 1929 caused many problems: water pipes froze and standpipes had to be erected, streams froze or were blocked by ice, causing flooding; even eggs in shops froze solid. High unemployment added to the hardship and Mr and Mrs J. Cox, butchers, of 4 The Pavement, South Street, gave 100 gallons of soup to local school children on several occasions.

Nos 1 and 2 The Pavement, South Street, 1937. T. Taylor & Sons' hardware shop, decorated to celebrate the Coronation. Founded in 1885 by Jonathan Taylor at No. 41 South Street, the shop is still run by the family, having moved to No 1 The Pavement in 1895. No. 2 was added in 1926 and the shop still occupies these premises.

Taylor & Son delivery van, *c.*1900. The van toured locally selling hardware, china, glass, and paraffin oil, which was in great demand for lighting and heating before the introduction of electricity.

41 South Street, 1915; White's Clock & Watch Shop, run by two Tom Whites from 1902 to 1967. Tom Snr came to Isleworth in 1899, opening his own business in 1902 at No. 41, where Tom Jnr was born. Tom Jnr became one of the country's most prominent horologists. He worked for Garrards of Regent Street, certified watches for Government, Police and Sports organisations and for 75 years cared for the clocks at Syon House.

43 South Street, 1915. Charlie Woods outside Woods tobacconist and confectionary shop. Charlie worked as a carver at The Mitre, Hampton Court, leaving his wife to run the shop. The Christmas window display includes stockings full of sweets, and advertises Rowntrees and Cadbury's chocolate, but who now remembers Rowney's pencils, Arnold's inks, or Rutter's tobaccos and snuff?

South Street, c.1910, facing the Twickenham Road. On the right, E. Goddards, bootmaker. Beyond, hardware hangs outside Denyers Oil and Colour Stores and in the distance can be seen the canopy of Balch's butchers. On the left, Costloe's Piano Warehouse with sheet music and records in the window. Next door, Star Supply Stores advertises 'Overweight – Margarine 8d. lb.' The billboards stand outside Burgess & Son, tobacconists and stationers (later Coates). The buildings on the right were demolished in 1957 to allow road widening – Wisdom Court flats replacing the shops.

Mr Ernest Templer Goddard with his wife, Alice, outside his bootmaker's shop at 64 South Street, 1910. Mr Goddard bought the business in 1893 having previously served an apprenticeship as improver to Mr Sherborne. The business later moved across the road to No. 43, Mr Goddard's son, Harry, having taken over the shop in 1925; he retired in 1974. Wisdom Court now covers the site of No. 64.

Mr Sidney Coates, printing works, 53 South Street, c.1925. Mr Coates took on the shop in 1922, first as a tobacconist and subsequently as a printer. In the doorways stands Mrs Tout, Mr Coates' daughter, and on the right, Alf Goode. Today the shop is still a printers although now run by the Self brothers, whose father, Mr Clifford Self, had acted as assistant to Mr Coates and took over the shop in 1942.

Isleworth carol party in the 1920s, photographed in the garden behind No. 78 South Street (R. Watts – hairdresser). The carol party collected 'in aid of Xmas treats for old people and poor children'. Among those shown are Mrs A. Goodard, Dick Watts, Harry Goddard, Percy Bell, 'Whitehaired Bob', and 'Nan' Bell. The pigeon loft stood in the garden of No. 76, owned by Mr Hazell.

Mrs Menzies, 'Ginger' Baker, and Cyril Davis are outside Parker's Stores at 77 South Street, 1915. A long, narrow shop with mahogany counter and shelves wgere bacon, cheese and butter were cut to order. Dried fruit, cereal, sugar and tea were sold loose in blue paper bags. Service was a byword and orders were delivered daily by horse van. Tinned goods in the window include pears, 9d., plums, 8d., sardines, 6d., salmon, 9/-, and trout, 6/-. The Kitchener-style poster proclaims 'Skipper Sardines – We've got em on toast'.

An impressive display of meat outside Balch's butchers at 74 South Street c.1905. John Balch, left of the doorway with his assistant Tom Layton on the right of the doorway and staff, all stand resplendent in their aprons with butcher's steels hanging at their waists. Above the distinctive canopy, fir trees proclaim this to be Christmas-time, when a policeman was hired to guard the shop overnight. Behind the shop stood a slaughterhouse.

South Street, winter 1957-8. On the left is the War Memorial at the Twickenham Road junction and Gumley House. Centre, St Bridget's Church; right, Wisdom Court, nearing completion. In 1957, shops and houses on the north side of South Street were demolished to make way for road widening. Two blocks of flats were built behind the new street line, Wisdom Court named after William Wisdom, a prominent local builder, and Swan Court named after Harold Swan, the former town clerk.

Two

Isleworth
The Extended Village

As the population in Isleworth grew, so the land immediately surrounding the village was gradually converted from agriculture to residential use with a corresponding development of services for the growing population – new shops, schools, churches. Industries like the brewery and Pears Soap factory increased employment opportunities, while the development of transport from horse to motorised vehicle, and also the railway, contributed to the change from village to suburb.

The junction of Twickenham Road and South Street in 1905; on the left is the site where St Bridget's Church was later built. Next, in South Street, J. Neville's greengrocery and Parker's Stores. To the right of Parker's Stores at No. 79, partially hidden by bushes, William Winterbourne, a notable local character ran an iron foundry. On the extreme right is the George Inn that dates from 1731, although it has been rebuilt since then. In the centre the Old Fire Station at The Mount.

The Clock Tower War Memorial, c.1928; 11.00am on 11 November, it is the minute's silence. The War Memorial was built at the junction of South Street and Twickenham Road, and was unveiled on 22 June 1922. The clock tower bears the names of 386 Isleworth men killed in the First World War, and also commemorates those killed during the Second World War. Behind can be seen St Bridget's Catholic Church and the Old Fire Station. The gallows-like structure was used to dry fire hoses.

Isleworth Fire Brigade, c.1904, posing with their new engine by the fire station at The Mount on the Twickenham Road near the present War Memorial. This building opened in 1887 and remained in use until 1937, when the fire station on the London Road opened. Before 1887, the engine was housed under one of the arches of the Old Blue School.

Our Lady of Sorrows and St Bridget's Catholic Church, Twickenham Road, 1912. In October 1907 Bishop Fenton laid the foundation stone of the church to be built on a site given by Miss Saunders. In October 1910, he returned to consecrate the completed church. The building was designed by F.D. Webb – after St Clement's in Rome – and has, unusually, a marble Baldachino over the high altar. In 1925, Viscount Fitzalan unveiled a war memorial in the church and in 1927 a tower was added. Before St Bridget's opened, local Catholics worshipped at a chapel in Shrewsbury Place.

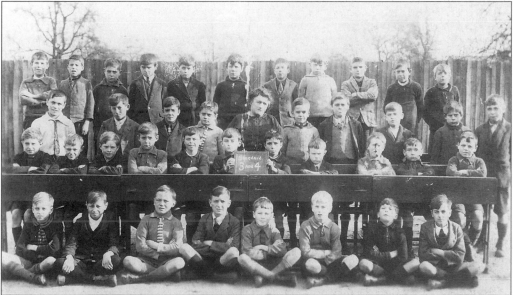

St Mary's Catholic Primary School, 3 November 1924. Mrs Gavan, the governess and wife of the headmaster, is shown with pupils who include, back row, left to right: 4. L. Hill, 6. F. Maley, 8, ? Collins, 9. ? Pollard, 10. ? Kirby, 11. ? Mason. Second row: 7. ? Sanderson, 9. ? Fullicks (?). Third row: 4. T. Murphy, 6. E. Taylor, 7. E. Lucas, 8. ? Meacock (?), 10. J. McCann (?). Front row: 2. ? Hicks, 3. ? Argent, 5. P. Weathers, 8. ? Lofting. A boys' school opened on the present St Mary's site in 1907. Girls were educated separately at a primary school attached to Gumley Secondary School. The two did not combine until 1948.

Convent F. C. J., Gumley House, Isleworth.

Gumley House convent and school, Twickenham Road, c.1910, built in the early eighteenth century for the wealthy glass manufacturer John Gumley. In 1841, Gumley House was sold to the Catholic Order of the Faithful Companions of Jesus, who developed the site as a convent with an attached girls' boarding school and day school. The enlarged school buildings now form a girls' comprehensive school.

Catholic Procession or Pilgrimage Isleworth 1916

Catholic procession, Twickenham Road, 1916. Part of the Catholic Martyrs procession passing the end of North Street – the whole procession was over half a mile long! In the centre background are the Sermons Almshouses and the glasshouses of Silverhall Nursery.

Sermons Almshouses, *c.*1970. Standing on the corner of Twickenham Road and North Street, these six almshouses were built and endowed in 1843 by Mrs Sarah Sermon.

Silverhall Nursery, 15 September 1899. Brothers Philip, Daniel and John Weathers with Dorothy and Maurice, children of John Weathers. John (1867-1928) trained at several gardens, including Kew, and became Assistant Secretary of the Royal Horticultural Society. Largely self-educated, he learned French, German and Latin, and wrote a number of gardening books. John ran the Silverhall Nursery on the Twickenham Road and took a prominent part in local affairs, notably as founder and editor of the *Isleworth Citizen Journal*.

Twickenham Road, 1912. On the left is the junction with North Street and the entrance to Sermon's Almshouses; the turning on the right is St John's Road, with the Duke of Cornwall on the corner. Further along, the tall building is Gumley House Convent and School and in the centre can be seen the Old Fire Station. Children are playing in the road, barefoot. Today, a mini roundabout controls this busy junction.

The junction of Twickenham Road and St John's Road, c.1920. Members of the Duke of Cornwall Darts Club are ready for an outing. This nineteenth-century public house was demolished in the 1960s and is now the offices of Barnett and Barnett, Insurance Brokers. The name possibly commemorated Richard, Earl of Cornwall (brother of Henry III), who once owned the Manor of Isleworth.

St John's Road from the Twickenham Road junction, *c*.1900; on the left is the corner of the Duke of Cornwall public house; further along, the building with the window on the side was the Isleworth Club and Institute, now Isleworth Working Men's Club and Institute. In the background can be seen the chimney and buildings of Isleworth Brewery.

Racking Room, Isleworth Brewery, in 1905. There has been a brewery in St John's Road since 1726, principally run by the Farnell family who sold the business to Watneys in 1923. Under Watneys, brewing stopped on the site, which became a bottling plant before closing altogether in 1992. The site is currently being redeveloped for housing. Note the long leather aprons and protective boots, also 'Isleworth Brewery Ltd' inscribed on the barrels, which were made on site.

Frozen river, February 1929. During the severe cold spell of February 1929, parts of the Duke of Northumberland's River froze. Here, 16 workmen from Isleworth Brewery stand on the ice. The brewery buildings can be seen in the background on the left, and behind the men can be seen the footbridge normally used to cross the water.

Isleworth Brewery Quoits Team in action, c.1925. The brewery, like other large employers, encouraged the sporting and social activities of its staff. Facilities were available for cricket, football, boxing, tennis, bowls, billiards, darts, tug-of-war, quoits, etc. Staff dances and dinners were held regularly, and the annual Isleworth Fun Day with sideshows, competitions, pageants, music, and fireworks, was eagerly anticipated throughout the year.

Brewery Sports Day in the 1930s. Top-hatted trainers Bill Hennesy and Jack Hopcroft pose for the cameraa before a 'dog' race. Judging by the chains, the hounds were ferocious animals! In the background the brewery yeast room is seen with interested onlookers, including Reg Field.

Isleworth Brewery Sports Day, 6 September 1930. Attractions included coconut shies, bowling for a live pig, sideshows, and a parade of employees on bicycles decorated to resemble aeroplanes of all ages, which ended in an 'aerial' battle with protagonists fighting until their cardboard machines disintigrated. Competitors included A. Wells (Amy Johnson), J. Hopcroft (R. 102), R. Field (Lindberg) and, pictured here, W. Benn (prehistoric aviator).

Isleworth Brewery Foden Steam Lorry, 1928. George T. Jones and Fred Humphries (driver) and two crew members with their lorry, photographed in Grainger Road. The cab was open, and the driver exposed to all weathers.

Grainger Road, 1953. Mrs Hilda Allnutt with children from Grainger Road at a street party celebrating the coronation of Queen Elizabeth II. Planks and beer crates help to form the seating, with flags, bunting, and paper hats to create a party spirit.

County High School, St John's Road, c.1905. Built in 1897 on land given by Andrew Pears, the County High School developed out of the Upper Department of the Blue School. In 1939, the school moved to a new site in Ridgeway Road, becoming Isleworth Grammar School (now Isleworth & Syon Comprehensive). The St John's Road building was later used as an annexe to Isleworth Polytechnic, subsequently as a community centre, and currently as a 'temporary' primary school.

Marholm Leys, St John's Road, 1928. Mr R.G. Brickner relaxes in the notable garden, which had been perfected by a former occupant, a dentist named Fritsch. The house was sold to developers in 1938, demolished, and St John's Court built on the site, fortunately completed before war broke out.

St John's Road, *c*.1850. The architect's drawing shows, clockwise: St John's Church, the Vicarage, Woodlands St John's School, and Farnell's Almshouses. Expanding population in the 1840s caused overcrowding at All Saints' Church and a new church was proposed as a solution. The Duke of Northumberland gave a site on St John's Road, and donated £2,000 towards the cost of construction, the balance being raised by the community. In 1855, the Duke laid the foundation stone and the church was consecrated in 1856. In 1857, St John the Baptist was created as a separate parish. Much of the money for the church was given by the Farnell and Glossop families. The vicarage, school, and almshouses were all the gift of Mr John Farnell, owner of the Isleworth Brewery, and the Farnell family crest is incoparated in each of these buildings. For many years, the almshouses were administered by the Brewery, and a bust of John Farnell by Henry George May, the local scupltor, stood over the well in the centre of the almshouses' courtyard. Before the construction of the church, St John's Road was called Brazil Mill Lane and a stream ran beside the road until early this century. A bridge crossing the stream can be seen to the bottom right of the drawing.

Woodlands St John's Infant School, 1922, erected in 1859 off St John's Road as the gift of Mr John Farnell, consisted of a school and adjoining school house. It closed in 1973 and the buildings are now private residences. Two of the girls are wrapped in scarves as a remedy for sore throats, and the boy in the front seems to have mumps or toothache!

St John's Church Girls' Guild. These are members of the Girls' Guild run by Miss Emerson at St John's Church, fund raising in 1917. 'Sargeant' Nellie Knight is shown with Kathleen Harstam, Ivy Phillipps, Mildred York, Amy Denyer, Kath Doughty, Hilda Voller, Dolly Lines, Phyllis Thompson, Mary Armes, Nellie Redknap, and Vi Portman.

Refreshments, St John's Vicarage, 1916. Tea on the Vicarage lawn, 1916 style. Among those serving tea at this fund-raising event are Mrs Donaldson Selby, who lived at the Vicarage, and Miss Dawes of Suffolk Lodge. They are seen together with other ladies from the congregation, and maid servants from the Vicarage including Emily Rapley. On the table are an urn, cakes, sponges, and china, while under the table are boxes, baskets, and baking trays.

Suffolk Lodge, Woodlands Grove, 1908. Built in 1857 as the country residence of Joseph Last, whose eleven-year-old niece laid the foundation stone. Joseph, a trunk-maker of Haymarket, originally came from Suffolk, hence the house's name. A later occupant was G.W. Dawes, JP, who presented the Dawes Cup to the Rowing Club. Subsequently, the house became an old people's home, then a guest house. It has since been demolished, but a modern block of flats on the site retains the name.

Woodlands Grove, early this century. The tall Laleham House (left) still stands, as do the other buildings. To the right, off the picture behind the walls, stood four houses, now replaced by Hawkfield Court, a block of thirty flats. In the distance can be seen Woodlands Road, and the tower of St John's Church.

Woodlands Road, 1909; to the left is the turning into Woodlands Grove. The building in the centre, Bedfont Lodge, has been demolished and replaced by modern flats which, however, retain the name. On the right stands St John's Lodge, and in the distance the tower of St John's Church is seen. The market gardens, behind the hedge in the right foreground, have been developed for housing.

Woodland Gardens in the early 1930s, built on land that was previously orchards and market gardens. Work commenced in 1928 and, when completed, a three-bedroomed, semi-detached house cost about £700. The turning on the right leads to Woodlands Road.

The Woodlands, 1907. On the extreme left is Woodlands Road. The building on the corner has now been demolished and replaced by flats, Riverside Court. The wooden bridge crossing the Duke of Northumberland's River led into fields where Octavia Road now stands.

Woodlands Road facing St John's Road, 1910. The two buildings on the extreme right, on the junction of the Woodlands, have now been demolished and a block of flats, Riverside Court, was erected in their place. The other buildings all survive. On the left, the group of chimneys marks the building now known as Kingswood Hotel.

St John's Road, c.1910. On the right is the junction of Woodlands Road with the Railway Inn (now renamed the Woodlands Tavern) on one corner, and a grocer's shop opposite. The branch post office opened in St John's Road in 1892 and was closed c.1925; the building has now been converted into shop premises.

St John's Road, 1925. On the left, on the corner of Loring Road, is Salter's Stores, advertising Oxo and gas mantles, and displaying buckets, brushes, and a tin bath. On the right, G. Hibbert's, the butcher's shop, is seen with meat and rabbits hanging in the open and sawdust strewn on the ground. Advertising State Express Cigarettes is S.H. Townsend, newsagent and tobacconist. Beyond can be seen the cobble-stones of Aylett Road, and the Railway Inn. In the distance the tower of St John's Church can be seen.

At the junction of Linkfield Road and Loring Road, 1911, James Smith's Hygienic Bakery. A bakehouse stood beside the shop, which had marble-topped counters. Wooden troughs were used for kneading the dough. Hand-made hot cross buns were only available on Good Friday, and deliveries were made by bicycle with a special storage box. Beyond the baker's, a barber's advertises a wash and brush-up for 2d.

68

The Red Lion public house in Linkfield Lane (now Road), 1887. This photograph was taken by a travelling photographer. Those appearing in the picture, from left to right, are: a character who scratched a living by trapping birds and rabbits on the market gardens (now Smallberry Avenue), his name unknown; Mr Bland, master baker, of Linkfield Road, and a child; Mr E.H. Steed of Worple Road; Mr Phil Woods of South Western Terrace; nurseryman from the nursery at the rear of the pub; a draper from South Street, name unknown; and the licensee, Mr Spurge.

Mrs Minnie Elizabeth Whenman, c.1910, one of the first certified midwives to work in Isleworth. Mrs Whenman (1870-1954) was a familiar figure at a time when large families were the norm and home births more common than today. She lived with her family in Linkfield Road.

Bell's Almshouses, Linkfield Road, 1973, built in 1822 as the Infirmary of the Parish Workshouse. The Infirmary was sold in 1839 when the new Union Workhouse was built and purchased by Isleworth Charity Trustees to house six unmarried or widowed women. A separate building, on the same site, provided housing for two married couples. These buildings replaced an earlier almshouse founded by the Misses Bell in 1739.

Rayment's Almshouses, Linkfield Road, 1973. The Almshouses were endowed by Samuel Rayment, who rose from baker's boy to become manager of the Isleworth Flour Mill. Rayment's Almshouses were built adjacent to Bell's Almshouses in 1936 to provide housing for two married couples of not less than 60 years of age. In 1975 both Rayment's and Bell's Almshouses were demolished and replaced by Raybell Court, a complex of 21 modern flats on the same site.

Linkfield Road, 30 July 1919. A procession of decorated cars, carts, traps, bicycles, etc., and people in fancy dress paraded through the district as part of the peace celebrations following the end of the First World War. Here, Isleworth fire crew pose for the camera on their Merryweather steam fire engine.

Peace celebrations, 30 July 1919. Winners of the Decorated Vehicle section in the Peace Parade. Throughout the district, houses and shops were decorated. Parades took place with marching bands; three thousand Isleworth children were fêted in Syon Park, and services of thanksgiving were held. Among those pictured with the cart in Steele Road are John Arnold, Liz Arnold, Mr Cook, Mrs Letherington, Mrs Gay, Mrs Cook, Maud Letherington, Ellen Mortimer, and Mr Letherington.

Worple Dairy Milk Float, c.1917. J. Arnold ran Worple Dairy from 14 Steele Road. Here, his daughter, May (Later Mrs Bigwood), is delivering milk, assisted by George Chadwick. 'Special cows kept for the Nursery' is proudly proclaimed on the float. As well as milk, cream, new-laid and country eggs, fresh and Dorset butter were available.

Isleworth Police, 1931, the staff photographed behind the Worple Road Police Station in the year the station closed. The building is now converted into flats.

The police station at junction of Worple Road and Byfield Road, 1900. The station was built in 1873 to replace the police houses in Church Street and Twickenham Road. Worple Road station had two cells and, in 1903, a staff of three sargeants and 17 men. The station closed in 1931 although, housing a siren it was used again during the war for civil defence purposes.

Pierrot Troupe, c.1920. Its members performed at the Public Hall, South Street, in aid of charity. The troupe was run by Miss Ivy Over, who was noted for singing items such as 'Dear Little Jam Face'. This photograph was taken in one of the houses on Byfield Road.

Isleworth and St Margaret's Rifle Club, 1912. Formed in 1909, the Club had a rifle range first in the Baths Hall and later at Worple Road School. Among those pictured are Dr Goodwin; Mr Pfeiffer, dentist; Mr G.E. Bate, headmaster; Mr E. Lines, journalist; and Mr Clayton, headmaster of Holm Court Truent School (now Garvins), with pupils from Holm Court, wearing caps, who were allowed to attend as a reward for good behaviour.

Worple Road School, March 1911. Girls' scarf drill, photographed by Mr Lugg, the headmaster. The teacher is Miss Saunders, and pupils include Dorothy Scott, Ivy Hazard, Gertie Evans, Beattie Mould, Gladys Willis, Hilda Cronshey, Nettie Gibbs, Dorothy Over, Mabel Neighbour, Hilda Burtenshaw, Rose Baldwin, Dorothy Millar, May Mower, Emmie Nottingham, Jessie Bartholomew, Violet Thatcher, Irene Tebbutt, Ada Chennel, Olive Headen, Amy Small, and Nancy Moore. Opened in 1897, Worple Road School closed in 1993, when it was replaced by the new Worple School in Queens Terrace.

Mr Alfred William Lugg (1871-1947), the headmaster of Worple Road Junior Mixed School from February 1906 until December 1935, when he retired. During the First World War he commanded the VAD at Percy House, and is shown here in 1916, photographed in his VAD uniform. He took a prominent part in local social and sports organsiations and was a player and captain for Brentford Football Club in the 1890s, before the Club turned professional. He was also involved with Isleworth Swimming Club, Hounslow Polytechnic Photographic Society, and Isleworth Aid and Welfare Society, as well as other organisations.

Percy House School, Twickenham Road, c.1910. The school was built in 1883 as a residential school for workhouse children and was successively used as a military hospital, a location for War Office records, and as an old people's home. Most of the buildings were demolished in 1978, one wing being retained by the West Middlesex Hospital. The site is currently (in 1995) being developed for housing.

Percy House School Band, 1907. Organised on military lines and led by Mr Theobalds, the band took part in many local events. The school stood opposite Isleworth Town School and in addition to dormitories and classrooms it contained a chapel, laundry, kitchens, a swimming bath, library, dining room, and workshops where pupils learned a trade. The boys were housed in a separate wing to the girls and the infants.

Percy House Hospital, Christmas 1916. In October 1915, Percy House was converted into an auxiliary military hospital with thirteen wards and an operating theatre. By December 1918, 4,989 men had been treated there.

Isleworth Voluntary Aid Detatchment, 1916. Members received first aid training and gave part-time voluntary service at Percy House Hospital. The Commandant, Mr A. Lugg, is seated right of Matron, and standing in the centre of the archway is Stanley Nixon, South Street photographer, who took this and many of the other photographs used in this book.

Twickenham Road, *c*.1910. The white-fronted building on the right is the Chequers Inn, demolished in 1933 when the present building was erected. On the left, behind the fence, was the Hospital Sports Field, now being developed for housing. In the centre can be seen the shops between Linkfield Road and St John's Road.

No. 197 Twickenham Road, *c*.1920, showing Arthur Scrivens Dairy, also known as Isleworth Creamery, advertising 'Absolutely pure new milk' as well as 'Nevill's bread at $7\frac{1}{2}$ d per loaf, and Nevill's pastry flour'. The window display shows a model milk churn, a few soda siphons, and the ubiquitous Aspidistras.

Twickenham Road, 1929. The stretch of Twickenham Road near the Linkfield Road Junction has always been liable to flooding. Here, flood water has dislodged the tar-coated wood blocks which formed the road surface, leaving a No. 67 tram stranded. The 67 tram ran from Hammersmith to Hampton Court from 1901-1935, when trolley buses took over the route. These ceased to run in 1962. The white-fronted building was the old Chequers public house, first recorded as licensed premises in 1731 and demolished in 1933. In 1929 the landlord, Mr Salter, had to call out the fire brigade to pump twelve feet of flood water from his cellars.

West Middlesex Hospital, *c*.1920. Twickenham Road runs left to top right. Rose and Crown Lane leads into Twickenham Road, with Thanet House at the junction, but the area is still undeveloped. On the right can be seen Park Road and the Cemetery.

West Middlesex Hospital Medical Staff, *c*.1925. Seated in second row, left to right: -?-, Dr Johnson, Sister Miller, Dr J.B. Cook (Medical Director 1911-1945), Miss E. Huggins (Matron 1915-1945), -?-, Dr Screech, -?-, and Theatre Sister.

Laundry Staff, West Middlesex Hospital, 1933. The Manageress, Mrs Austin (seated, wearing a cap) is pictured with 35 members of the hospital laundry staff. At that time laundry was done on the premises. Today, hospital laundry is contracted out and none is done on site. The names of all the staff in the photograph are known; back row, left to right: Vi Fields, Alice Barratt, Ada Warrel, Elsie Kilner, Rose Farrow, Annie Dargon, Mrs Kearney. Second row: Glad Wardon, Kate Jackson, Minnie Jackson, Joan Farrow, Annie Clements, Liz Barratt, Ivy Hatherall. Third row: Rose Bolton (standing), Vi Goldthorpe, May Shortland, Lil Saunders, Sally Tyler, Vi Fountain, Elsie Aspinall, Mrs Whiteman, Mrs Wakefield, Mrs Hursey, Mr Williams (washhouse man). Fourth row: Lou Bristow, Ivy James, Lil Delabar, Mrs Austin (manageress), Mrs Knowles (forewoman), Flo Newsome, Mrs Danibar, Lizzie Lawton. Front row: Tom Slater (washhouse man), Vi Clements, Annie Hipwell.

First Aid Post, Busch Corner, 1942. During the war, first aid posts like this provided emergency treatment for casualties. Hurricane lamps provided lighting and medical equipment is basic, but a teapot and urn stand ready to provide comfort. Behind, Busch Corner Health Clinic can be seen, which closed in 1991 and has since been demolished.

Domestic science lesson at The Green School for Girls, 1934. Originally founded in 1796 as a Church Sunday School, it became a day school in 1823 with premises in Park Road from 1859. The Green School moved to its present Busch Corner site in 1906, when it opened as a grammar school. In July 1934 new buildings were opened, which were later severely damaged in the war. The buildings have since been restored and extended.

Green School, 1931. Members of Elm House with House Captain I. Hewitt and Vice-Captain D. Lidbetter together with second mistress, Miss Mackie. Like most schools, the Green School was divided into houses to encourage competition among pupils. Those at the Green School were named after trees in the school grounds: elm, beech, chestnut, and oak.

Marlborough School, 1952, the participants in a staff versus pupils hockey match. The teachers, standing left to right, are: Miss Mallett, Mrs Kaye, Mrs Pilly, Miss Gee, Miss McGuinn, Mrs Everette, Miss Adlam, Miss Huggins, Miss Hammond, Miss Brown, and Miss Botting. It was built in 1932 as a co-educational school, but became a girls' school in 1939 when the boys moved to Smallberry Green School. Marlborough School closed in 1968 and was subsequently used as an employment training centre, but has now been demolished for housing.

Pears Factory, London Road, c.1915. The factory was built between 1880 and 1884 to replace older works on the opposite side of the road. Pears soap was produced here until 1962. The factory has now been demolished, and Western Atlas occupies the site. Pears' hooter was a recognised local time signal – there was consternation on the day the hooter failed! Smells of perfume, wafting from the factory, are remembered by many local residents.

Pears Factory, 1953, workers processing application forms for a special offer promoted by a national newspaper in celebration of the coronation of Queen Elizabeth II.

War work at Pears Factory, *c*.1943. Many local factories contributed to the war effort. Here, seals on aircraft fuel tanks are being tested by Norah Newton, Ivy Norman, and Julie May.

Empire Day, *c*.1905. Crowds gather on Pears Field (now Sidmouth Avenue) to celebrate Empire Day. Sporting contests, among many events, were popular. Here, a tug of war is the centre of attention.

Empire Day *c*.1905. Inaugurated in 1902 and held on 24 May to honour Queen Victoria's birthday, Empire Day was celebrated with patriotic fervour. This stall has been decorated with a banner and flags, and the ladies are all wearing their Sunday best with magnificent hats.

London Road, c.1965; on the right, the Rising Sun public house; on the left, Frazer Nash, for many years a garage, car showroom and racing car workshop. Royal Naval mechanics were trained here during the Second World War. Note the 'tardis' police box.

Flooding, London Road, 19 June 1914. The iron bridge on the London Road was erected in 1850, when the railway extended to Isleworth. The dip under the bridge has always been liable to flooding. The Iron Bridge Tavern on the corner of Linkfield Road was also built in 1850 for William Farnell of the Isleworth Brewery. The wall marked 'Pears' stands outside the Pears soap factory.

Isleworth Station, *c.*1900. In 1850, Isleworth Station opened, replacing Smallberry Green (a temporary station further east) as the terminus of the London and South Western Railway's Barnes–Isleworth loop line. This line now extends to Hounslow. For many years the station was known as Spring Grove Station.

Isleworth Station, *c.*1900. Today, the neat fencing has gone. The station forecourt is a car park with newspaper, bottle and can banks, and a SuperLoo. The station, which had 16 staff in 1880, is now unmanned, and in 1995 the weather-boarded station office (left of picture) was demolished. At least the trains still run!

Kings Parade, London Road, 1910. Built to supply the needs of houses in Spring Grove, shops in Kings Parade included a draper, hosier, cobbler, dairy, greengrocer, tobacconist, hairdresser, fishmonger/poulterer, butcher, jeweller, newsagent, upholsterer, seed merchant, hardware, furniture and cycle shops, and tea room. Shops co-operated over advertising and delivery and there was one telephone number for all orders. The draper and novelty shop seen right on the corner of St John's Road is now a bank.

No. 483 London Road, c.1930. F. Fenn & Son, Watchmakers and Jewellers. The road has been renumbered and the shop front altered since the photograph opposite, dating from 1913, was taken, but the shop is on the same site. In 1995 the third and fourth generations of the family continue to run the business.

No. 5 Kings Parade, London Road, 1913: F. Fenn, Watchmaker and Jeweller. Frederick Fenn established the shop on this site in 1910.

Kings Parade, London Road, 1910, looking towards Hounslow. Avenue Road is on the right and St John's Road on the left, level with the tram. Today, above the shop fronts, the buildings are largely unaltered but the shop fronts, the road surface, and the traffic are now very different.

PC Peter James Mate, c.1850, joined the force on 13 January 1840. He was on 'T' Division for his whole term of service; he was based locally and was reputedly one of the first uniformed police constables in the area. After retirement on 10 August 1864 aged 50 – because of chronic rheumatism – he lived at 8 Toynes Cottages, London Road. On his retirement he was given a certificate '2' for good conduct. He died on 20 November 1877 in the Union Workhouse.

Three

Spring Grove, Osterley and Wyke

North of the London Road, set in agricultural land, stood a few scattered hamlets and several large estates. In 1850, Henry Daniel Davies purchased the Spring Grove Estate – once home to Sir Joseph Banks – and began to develop housing for the prosperous Victorian middle classes. A second wave of development followed the opening of the Great West Road in 1925, Although Osterley House and its estate fortunately escaped developers and is now a National Trust property. Wyke House was not so fortunate and both house and grounds are now replaced by modern housing. All this land north of the London Road was originally in the ancient parish of Heston, although it had close ties with Isleworth.

Spring Grove House, pictured in 1917, was used during the First World War as a hospital for members of Queen Mary's Army Auxiliary Corps. It was equipped with an operating theatre and had a staff of 57, including three doctors. Convalescent WAACs were able to relax in the grounds and various recreation facilities were available for them – including the use of a gramophone given by Queen Mary.

The art room, Isleworth Polytechnic School, 1959. Middlesex County Council purchased Spring Grove House in 1922 for educational purposes, and in 1923 Spring Grove Grammar School opened. The school moved to Lampton in 1959 when the buildings were used by the Isleworth Polytechnic, which later became Hounslow Borough College. Today, it is West Thames College.

Harry Goddard's Rhythm Dance Band in the 1920s, performing at a May Fair held in the grounds of Spring Grove House. Playing the piano is Miss Theresa Costloe (the Costloe Piano Warehouse was at 49 South Street), Harry Goddard (bootmaker of 64 South Street) is playing the banjulele, and Percy Godsell is on the drums. The child's name is not known.

The Lodge, The Grove, *c.*1920. Built for Andrew Pears to serve as the main entrance to Spring Grove House, the Lodge bears the initials A.P. and the date 1893. Harvard Road had not then been built, and the land between Harvard Road and the Grove was still part of the Spring Grove House estate.

The junction of The Grove and London Road, 1916. The pillars were erected when Mr Henry Daniel Davies was developing Spring Grove, to mark the entrance to the estate. They were removed in 1965 to facilitate road widening.

The junction of Spring Grove Road and London Road, 1909. Andrew Pears presented the drinking fountain and water trough to the residents of Heston and Isleworth in 1899. It was removed in the 1930s when it was found to cause traffic congestion. The copse to the left of the picture is the site where Heston and Isleworth Fire Station was built in 1937.

London Road, c.1935. Spring Grove Road leads off to the right with Pears Fountain in the middle of the junction. The buildings in this parade, erected in 1887, have altered little, although the shop fronts have changed greatly.

London Road, *c*.1935. On the right the Milford Arms stands on the corner of Thornbury Road, advertising billiards, pool, and pyramids as attractions. (Pyramids is a game played on a billiard table). Apart from the lack of traffic and the size of the trees, this scene has altered little.

London Transport, Isleworth depot, London Road, 1962. The depot was built in 1901 for London United Tramways Company as a ten-track tram depot with adjoining electricity sub-station. The depot was enlarged and largely rebuilt in the 1930s following the switch to trolleybuses. London Transport closed the depot in 1962. It has since been used as a Post Office transport depot and is currently a storage facility.

Overton House, London Road, in the snow, 1930. Now demolished, the house stood opposite Kings Parade. The nearby Overton Close commemorates its name. Dr Frank Dendle once lived here; in addition to his general practice he was Medical Officer to Borough Road Training College and Divisional Surgeon to the Police. The site is now occupied by an office block.

London Road, c.1905, showing the stretch of road opposite the Kings Parade shops with the Avenue Road junction in the centre of the picture. The railway bridge can be seen behind the coachman and the turret on Beechen Cliff centre right. Note the condition of the road surface, the tram lines and cables. Trams first used this road in July 1901, running between Kew Bridge and Hounslow.

Beechen Cliff, No. 452 London Road, c.1977. This house stood at the junction with College Road and is seen from College Road. Once known as 'Thistle Bon', the house was one of many large, ornate family houses in Spring Grove that have either been demolished or converted into flats. For some years Beechen Cliff was used as accommodation for nursing sisters from the West Middlesex Hospital, but it has now been demolished and Beechen Cliff Way stands on the site.

Mr Arthur Bond with his wife and shop assistant stand outside his coffee and dining rooms at 420 London Road, c.1910. No fast food or take-away then; dining rooms like this provided food on the premises. On offer were bloaters, haddock, eggs and bacon, kippers, and pea soup. It was named 16 South Western Terrace when it was first built (after the adjacent railway) but the Parade was later renumbered as part of London Road.

Marsden's Nursery, Rose Cottage, Wood Lane, *c.*1914. Among the staff shown outside Marsden's Nursery are Jim Voller, Billy Earle, Seth Voller, Abraham Voller, Fred Voller, Henry Marsden (owner of the Nursery) and 'Old Scheffer'.

Quakers Lane, 1910. Although much altered now, this is one of the few survivors of the many footpaths which criss-crossed Isleworth when much of the land was used for farms and market gardens. The name is derived from the nearby Friends' Meeting House. The Friends' Meeting House was built in 1785, although Quaker meetings had been held locally from 1659.

The bridge, Osterley Park, 1900. It was designed by William Chambers for Francis Child and built in the 1750s. Water no longer flows under the bridge, which lies stranded in farmland, ivy covering its 'Piranesian cyclopic rustication' [Pevsner].

Military Funeral, 1915. Several soldiers died while stationed at Osterley Park. In the funeral shown here, the coffin, draped with the Union Jack, was taken from Hounslow Barracks to Heston Churchyard on a horse-drawn gun carriage preceded by a military band, with an escort of troops. Following the committal, a salute was fired over the grave and the last post sounded by buglers.

Jersey Road, 1916. Between 1915 and 1918 the Army Service Corps had a training camp based in Osterley Park. Recruits were taught driving and vehicle maintenance, some of the instruction being given by London Bus drivers and using local roads. Facilities were basic, but local volunteers helped run a YMCA tent to provide some comforts. Here, seven trainees pose with their instructor and lorry in Jersey Road.

Witham Road, 1913. On the left is Burlington House, once a private school – Burlington Lodge Academy – where Robert Louis Stevenson was, in 1863, briefly and unhappily a pupil. Early this century it became the administrative headquarters of the Catholic Order of St Vincent de Paul and was accordingly renamed St Vincent de Paul. The house was demolished in 1966. St Vincent's Church was built on an adjoining site in 1935.

Colonel H.R. Peake, 1854-1933. Hugh Rossindel Peake grew up in Spring Grove, where his family lived, and was educated at T. Wyatt's School in Witham Road, before going to Tonbridge School. He entered the 2nd Volunteer Batallion of the Middlesex Regiment, rising through the ranks to be appointed Colonel in 1906, and was awarded the Volunteer Decoration. However, he is best remembered as: a solicitor, Clerk to the Isleworth Blue School Governors, Clerk to the Isleworth Charity Trustees (40 years), Clerk to the Heston and Isleworth Local Board (19 years), member of Heston and Isleworth Urban District Council (11 years), Heston School Board Clerk, Heston Vestry Clerk, Clerk to the Heston Charity Trustees (17 years), and Hon. Secretary of Hounslow Hospital (20 years). He died on 6 December 1933, and is buried at Heston.

Spring Grove Central School, Thornbury Road, 1934. Among those photographed are, back row: -?- , Sybil Grimmett, Winnie Syred, Annie Hayes, Minnie Batten, Marjorie Burton, Olive Pike, Hilda Titchmarsh, -?-. Middle row: Irene Tarrant, Hilda Prout, -?- Mr G.E. Bate, headmaster (and author of *And So Make A City Here*, a history of the local area), Miss Eva, Kathleen Carey, -?-, -?-. Front row: -?-, -?-, -?-, Daphne Cottrell. Although only girls are shown, the school was co-educational.

The back view of Campion House, Thornbury Road, c.1926, originally known as Thornbury House and built in 1856 as the home of Henry Daniel Davies (the speculative builder who developed much of Spring Grove). In 1911 it became a house of retreat for Catholic men, being renamed Campion House in 1915. In 1919 Campion House became a college run by the Jesuit Order, dedicated to training men with late vocations to the Priesthood. Since 1919, nearly 1,400 Campion House students have become priests.

Campion House students planting potatoes, c.1950. For many years Campion House students grew nearly all of the fruit and vegetables they required.

Thornbury Road, 1916. The building behind the long wall is Honnor's Home, built in 1860 as almshouses for the Saddler's Company, sold in 1903 and converted into flats called Osterley Mansions. The message on this postcard reads, 'You ought to be hear to see the aeroplanes I see three and four up together and there as been to operation bloons up'. Today, the wonder and excitement has vanished given our proximity to Heathrow!

Clifton House, Thornbury Road, 1905, showing Mr and Mrs Robert Tyler with their household staff. Many of the large houses in Spring Grove were run by a staff of live-in servants. The house was later the residence and surgery of Dr Robert Serjeant.

Chess Club, *c*.1915, Osterley residents who met to play chess. Standing, left to right: Mr A. Embleton; Mr A.L. Lang, architect; Mr G. Cutler, Hounslow jeweller; Mr Virgo, Hounslow Cycle Shop owner; Mr C. Wood, headmaster of Spring Grove Grammar School from 1923 to 1935. Seated: Mr J. Chesterman-Smith, journalist; Mr W. Hayward Young, an artist known as 'Jotter' who produced hundreds of scenic picture postcards; Mr C. Spink, West End butcher; and Dr R. Serjeant, who practised in Thornbury Road.

College Road, 1926, showing, on the left, Aysgarth, once the home of Charles Wood, the first headmaster of Spring Grove Grammar School and principal of the Polytechnic. To the right can be seen the fork of College Road and Ridgeway Road. Grove Road, to the left, was once called Favilla Road.

Spring Grove Primary School, 1906. Pictured are the headmaster, Mr A.E. Pope, and School Prize winners including W. Shirley, ? Bell, ? Podger, ? Poulton, S. Voller, F. Ravenhill, F. Voller, R. Hodges, ? Pallier, and trainers Mr Dew and Mr G. Hughes. Opening in Clifton Road in 1859 as a National School, Spring Grove Primary moved to new buildings in Star Road in 1965. The old buildings continued to house a playgroup and youth club, but were destroyed by fire in 1970 and housing now occupies the site.

Highfield Road, c.1910, largely unchanged today. In the distance, houses in College Road can be seen and in the foreground cabbages and leeks grow where the houses in Ridgeway Road now stand.

Osterley Road from The Grove, 1904. The building on the far right has now been demolished. During the Second World War, the Duchess of Gloucester Home for Disabled Servicemen was built on a site which extended between here and Ridgeway Road. Today, Isleworth Crown Court occupies the site. Railings seen in the middle distance border the cabbage field which became Isleworth Grammar School Sports Field. The spire of St Mary's Church is in the distance.

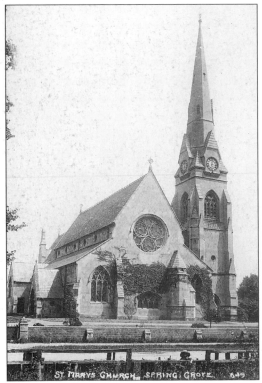

St Mary's Church, Spring Grove, 1904. The church was consecrated in December 1856 having been built at a cost of £15,000, entirely financed by Henry Daniel Davies, who had developed the Spring Grove estate. The site formed part of the grounds of Thornbury House (now Campion House), which was Mr Davies' residence, and the architect was John Taylor Jnr, who had designed many houses in Spring Grove for Mr Davies. In 1861, the original spire blew down during a storm – fortunately missing the church – and when the replacement was similarly damaged in 1867 it was decided to lower the spire some twelve feet.

Great West Road, *c*.1935, opened on 30 May 1925. Housing and factories quickly developed along the Great West Road. In the distance can be seen the landmark tower of Osterley Underground Station, built in 1934 and designed by S.A. Heaps and Charles Holden.

The Library at Borough Road Training College, *c*.1905. Joseph Lancaster, the pioneering educationalist, founded a teacher training college in Borough Road, Southwark, in 1810. In 1890 the College moved to new premises in Osterley with Borough Road being named after the College. It subsequently became part of the West London Institute of Higher Education, and now forms part of Brunel University College (Osterley Campus). Many students had their first practical teaching experience in local schools.

Osterley Hotel, 1928. Following the opening of the Great West Road, the Osterley Hotel was built at the Wood Lane junction.

The Rockery, Osterley Gardens, 1939. Opened on 18 July 1931, today the trees and plants are well established and the rocks blend into the landscape, but the shelter has now been burned down.

Great West Road from the north, 1932. To the bottom right are the Osterley Hotel and Wood Lane. Syon Lane crosses the Great West Road (top left) with Isleworth Winery at the junction. Opposite, Gillett's factory has yet to be built. On the extreme left is Macfarlane Lang's factory, and in the centre, Syon Park Gardens are under construction. Opposite, St Francis' Church and the surrounding housing have yet to be built. Across the foreground are the walled gardens of Wyke House.

Wyke House, c.1920. Dating from 1778 and the ownership of John Robinson, MP, who altered a much older house, the building shown was successively used and adapted as a family home, boys' school, and private asylum. The house eventually became derelict and was demolished in October 1977, despite local efforts to save it and aquire a Listed Building status. The site has since been developed for housing.

Garden staff at Wyke House, *c.*1905. Front left is George Daniel Manning, head gardener. Standing, on the left, is George Hurst, houseman and gardener at Wyke for over thirty years. He retired in 1936, when he lost his sight.

George Daniel Manning, *c.*1890; he was Head Gardener at Wyke House and is shown at Wyke wearing boots and spurs, astride a pig. The pig seems unconcerned, more interested in the contents of the trough!

Wyke House, *c.*1890. Staff and patients photographed in the ballroom at a Christmas fancy dress party. Matron is seated in the ornate chair. Minnie Bloomfield (nurse) is immediately to the right of Matron, and Henry Whenman is in the tall conical hat.

The Hare and Hounds, Windmill Lane, in the 1960s. It was built in 1904 to replace an eighteenth-century inn, which survived until it was demolished in 1958.

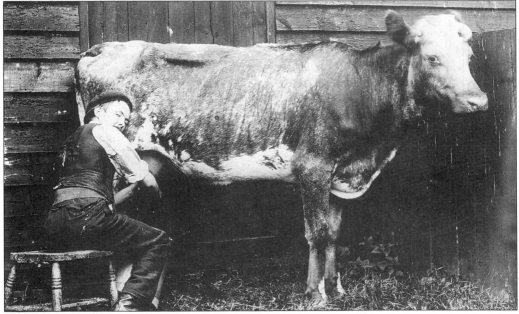

Mr Andrews and cow, Windmill Lane, c.1900. The cow was owned by the landlord of the Hare and Hounds and was kept at Wyke Farm. Twice a day the cow was led across the road to be milked in the presence of the landlord, who wanted his full quota of milk!

Four
Mogden and Worton

Mogden and Worton were two outlying hamlets set in large expanses of agricultural land. Gradually, through this century, the land use has changed from agricultural to residential with the larger houses either falling into disrepair and being demolished, like Worton Manor, or changing from residential to commerical use, like Worton Hall.

Worton Hall Film Studio staff, *c.*1920. In 1913 Worton Hall was purchased by London Film Productions Ltd. Film studios were built in the grounds of the Hall. *The African Queen* was the most notable film produced by 'Isleworth Studios'! The staff shown here were the carpenters, painters, and scene shifters in the studios.

The machine room, Worton Hall, *c.*1960. In 1952 the National Coal Board bought Worton Hall for use as a a mining research establishment. New tools and safety equipment was developed here for use throughout the country. The Coal Board closed the Hall in 1969. It has since become a trading estate.

Worton Manor, 1913. Built in the eighteenth century and enlarged in the ninenteenth, Worton Manor stood north of Worton Road near the Bridge Road junction. After many years of neglect it was demolished in about 1980. The Manor of Worton predates this building and was once owned by Syon Monastery.

The Labouring Boys, Worton Road, 1938. The buildings to the right formed the original Labouring Boys, which can be traced to a beerhouse on this site in the early nineteenth century. In 1938, the new building (centre of the picture) was erected behind the old, which was then demolished to provide car parking space.

Mrs Hettie Hill and her second son, Ernest, are outside the family tobacconist/confectionary shop at 3 Redlees Cottages, Worton Road, 1923. Mrs Hill also provided teas to cricket players in Redlees Park (9d per head) and during the Second World War cooked meals for troops manning the ack-ack battery in Redlees Park.

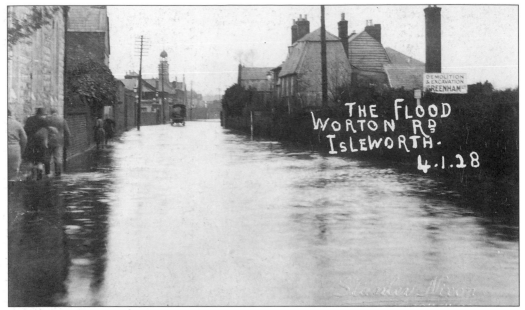

Flooding, Worton Road, 4 January 1928. Widespread flooding occurred in the area in early January 1928, when heavy rainfall, combined with thawing snow, raised the level of the Duke of Northumberland's River. On the left can be seen the Congregational Church and in the distance the clock tower on the stable block at Redlees and, right, Worton Cottage. Debenham's Nursery, behind the hedge, is now Gumley School playing fields. Eighteen inches of water in Worton Road forced residents to move upstairs.

Congregational Church, 1905, which was built as an independent church in 1848 at the corner of Worton Road and Twickenham Road and is now affiliated to the Congregational Federation. The rooms behind the church were formerly used as a British School.

Isleworth Congregational Church Band of Hope, *c*.1905. The Band of Hope was founded as part of the nationwide temperance movement that crusaded against the evils of alcohol. members, often children as young as eight, were expected to sign a pledge of abstinence since, as the motto on the banner proclaims, 'Prevention is better than cure'.

Jolly Gardeners, Twickenham Road, early 1920s, when the public house was a Royal Brewery House – the Royal Brewery on Brentford High Street was demolished in 1926. A 1924 advertisement for the Jolly Gardeners promoted 'Wireless Concerts nightly'.

Twickenham Road, 1953, and children are gathered outside the Jolly Gardeners for a party to celebrate the Coronation. Best party dresses, clean white socks, and paper hats – but where have all the boys gone? Were they sent home for being naughty, or did they have a separate party?

Mogden House, 1902. Arthur, Herbert, Amy, Edith, George and William Tebbutt outside Mogden House at the end of the Boer War, hence the flag. Built in the eighteenth century, Mogden House was the centre of Mogden House Nurseries, which operated until 1993. The house has since been converted into two units and the nurseries developed for housing; the new road is named Bankside Close.

Machinery at Mogden Purification Works, c.1938. When opened in 1936 as part of the wider West Middlesex Drainage Scheme, Mogden was the largest purification works in the world. It replaced twenty eight separate sewage works and served an area of 160 square miles covering seven boroughs and eight urban districts.

South Middlesex Hospital, c.1938. At the top of the picture runs Mogden Lane with, top left, the bank surrounding Mogden Water Works. To the left winds Rugby Road, and on the right is Hospital Lane and the orchards now replaced by the Ivybridge Estate. To the centre is South Middlesex Hospital built in 1938 as an isolation hospital, subsequently used to house elderly patients, and closed in 1990. The site is now a supermarket and housing estate.

Winter ploughing at Longschott, mid-1930s. Longschott was a 14½ acre field bounded by Mogden Lane, Whitton Dene and Hall Road that belonged to W.T. Mann and Sons of Oak Farm, Worton Road. Arnold Crescent now covers the site. Mr Harry Florey Snr, ploughman and carter for Manns, is shown with horses Prince and Flower. In the background is the bank around Mogden Purification Works.

Summer cultivation at Longschott, late 1930s. Mr Harry Florey Snr is using a multiple row seed-drill to plant a crop – probably lettuces or radishes. In the centre background is Twickenham Rugby Ground and in the right background is Truscow's Concrete Product Works, where Regency Mews now stands.

Five

St Margaret's

St Margaret's lies between Isleworth and Twickenham, although today, following the change of the borough boundary, it is part of the borough of Richmond. Historically, much of the area was in Isleworth and All Souls' was built as a daughter church of All Saints'. Old postcards of the Lock and Weir show the 'disputed' nature of the area, for they are captioned 'The Lock and Weir', 'Isleworth', 'St Margaret's', or 'Richmond', seemingly at a whim.

'Lock Bridge Isleworth-on-Thames', c.1910, officially known as Richmond Lock and Weir. The lock bridge was opened on 19 May 1894 when a toll of 1d was charged to cross the footbridge over the weir, but this was abolished in 1938. Pleasure craft still use this stretch of river, but now power boats have largely replaced the steam and rowing boats seen here.

Isleworth Promenade, c.1905. This Thames-side footpath, running from Railshead Road to St Margaret's Drive, has long been popular for angling, cycling, leisurely walking, or feeding the wild birds. To the right can be seen Isleworth Ait, and in the distance the wharves at Isleworth. Where the leisure boats are moored is now Thistleworth Marina houseboat mooring. The riverside edge of the promenade now has railings for public safety.

Railshead Ferry, 1908, established in the reign of George III. Railshead Ferry crossed the Thames by Railshead Road, near where the River Crane joins the Thames. The Ferry ceased to operate during the Second World War, after the Lock Bridge ceased to charge tolls. Compared with the previous photograph taken at the same spot, the tidal fall can clearly be seen.

St Margaret's Drive, *c.1925*. Members of Isleworth Rowing Club, fund raising for a local hospital at a Boxing Day Charity Regatta. Behind can be seen Kilmorey House, built in 1852 for the Earl of Kilmorey and from 1856 the home of the Royal Naval Female School. The school moved in 1941 following incendiary bomb damage to the house, which was demolished in 1945. The site is now part of Brunel University College.

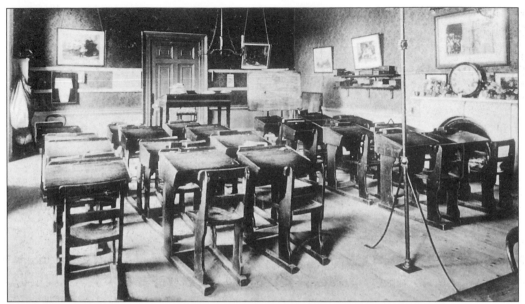

Royal Naval Female School Classroom, c.1905. The school occupied Kilmorey House from 1856 to 1941, with Gordon House added in 1922 as a 'Junior House'. Conditions at the school were Spartan, the girls rising at 6.15am and often complaining of the cold. Discipline was strict and the curriculum was quite advanced, including the French and German languages and Swedish drill.

L.C.C. Gordon House Girls' School, Isleworth.   Johnston Series.

Gordon House river front, 1905. Built in the seventeenth century with later additions, including work by Robert Adam, Gordon House had several notable residents including Moses Hart, General H. Bland, and the author Thomas Chandler Haliburton, before becoming the first London County Council Industrial School for girls in 1897. In 1922 the Industrial School closed and the house was acquired by the Royal Naval Female School who already occupied the adjacent Kilmorey House.

Gordon House garden front, 1965. In 1949 Gordon House became the home of Maria Grey College – founded in 1878 in Bishopsgate as a teacher training college. New buildings have been added as the college has expanded, and today the site is still used for higher education, although it now called Brunel University College.

All Souls' Church, c.1910. A temporary 'iron' church was opened in Northcote road in 1886 when a new parish was formed out of All Saints' parish in order to serve the increasing local population. Foundations for a permanent building were laid on 3 October 1896 and this building was consecrated on 2 January 1898. The iron church subsequently served as a church hall.

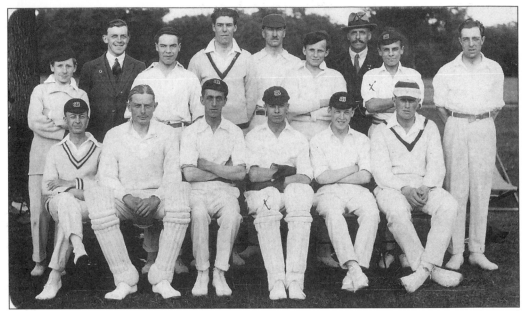

All Souls' Cricket Club, c.1920, when matches were played at Moormead Recreation Ground and Marble Hill Park. Seated, left to right: George Meeks, Revd M.W. Cuthbert (Curate, All Souls'), Arthur Tark, Bill Pearce, Fred Tidy, Tom Stoddart. Standing, left to right: 'Finger' Harding, Jack Sharp (scorer), John Pulsford, Tom Purvey, John or Bobby Scott (one of Dr Scott's sons), Len Lambard, Bill Pearce (Umpire), Walter Pearce, and an unknown person.

All Souls' Boy Scouts and Cubs, c.1915. Founded in Britain in 1908, the Scouting movement was encouraged by many churches because it provided organised leisure activities and developed character. The All Souls' troop is shown here with their standard and musical instruments.

Stock List

(Titles are listed according to the pre-1974 county boundaries)

BERKSHIRE

Wantage
Irene Hancock
ISBN 0-7524-0146 7

CARDIGANSHIRE

Aberaeron and Mid Ceredigion
William Howells
ISBN 0-7524-0106-8

CHESHIRE

Ashton-under-Lyne and Mossley
Alice Lock
ISBN 0-7524-0161 5

Around Bebington
Pat O'Brien
ISBN 0-7524-0121-1

Crewe
Brian Edge
ISBN 0-7524-0052-5

Frodsham and Helsby
Frodsham and District Local History Group
ISBN 0-7524-0161-0

Macclesfield Silk
Moira Stevenson and Louanne Collins
ISBN 0-7524-0315 X

Marple
Steve Cliffe
ISBN 0-7524-0316-8

Runcorn
Bert Starkey
ISBN 0-7524-0025-8

Warrington
Janice Hayes
ISBN 0-7524-0040-1

West Kirby to Hoylake
Jim O'Neil
ISBN 0-7524-0024-X

Widnes
Anne Hall and the Widnes Historical Society
ISBN 0-7524-0117-3

CORNWALL

Padstow
Malcolm McCarthy

ISBN 0-7524-0033-9

St Ives Bay
Jonathan Holmes
ISBN 0-7524-0186-6

COUNTY DURHAM

Bishop Auckland
John Land
ISBN 0-7524-0312-5

Around Shildon
Vera Chapman
ISBN 0-7524-0115-7

CUMBERLAND

Carlisle
Dennis Perriam
ISBN 0-7524-0166-1

DERBYSHIRE

Around Alfreton
Alfreton and District Heritage Trust
ISBN 0-7524-0041-X

Barlborough, Clowne, Creswell and Whitwell
Les Yaw
ISBN 0-7524-0031-2

Around Bolsover
Bernard Haigh
ISBN 0-7524-0021-5

Around Derby
Alan Champion and Mark Edworthy
ISBN 0-7524-0020-7

Long Eaton
John Barker
ISBN 0-7524-0110-6

Ripley and Codnor
David Buxton
ISBN 0-7524-0042-8

Shirebrook
Geoff Sadler
ISBN 0-7524-0028-2

Shirebrook: A Second Selection
Geoff Sadler
ISBN 0-7524-0317-6

DEVON

Brixham
Ted Gosling and Lyn Marshall
ISBN 0-7524-0037-1

Around Honiton
Les Berry and Gerald Gosling
ISBN 0-7524-0175-0

Around Newton Abbot
Les Berry and Gerald Gosling
ISBN 0-7524-0027-4

Around Ottery St Mary
Gerald Gosling and Peter Harris
ISBN 0-7524-0030-4

Around Sidmouth
Les Berry and Gerald Gosling
ISBN 0-7524-0137-8

DORSET

Around Uplyme and Lyme Regis
Les Berry and Gerald Gosling
ISBN 0-7524-0044-4

ESSEX

Braintree and Bocking
John and Sandra Adlam and Mark Charlton
ISBN 0-7524-0129-7

Ilford
Ian Dowling and Nick Harris
ISBN 0-7524-0050-9

Ilford: A Second Selection
Ian Dowling and Nick Harris
ISBN 0-7524-0320-6

Saffron Walden
Jean Gumbrell
ISBN 0-7524-0176-9

GLAMORGAN

Around Bridgend
Simon Eckley
ISBN 0-7524-0189-0

Caerphilly
Simon Eckley
ISBN 0-7524-0194-7

Around Kenfig Hill and Pyle
Keith Morgan
ISBN 0-7524-0314-1

The County Borough of Merthyr Tydfil
Carolyn Jacob, Stephen Done and Simon Eckley
ISBN 0-7524-0012-6

Mountain Ash, Penrhiwceiber and Abercynon
Bernard Baldwin and Harry Rogers
ISBN 0-7524-0114-9

Pontypridd
Simon Eckley
ISBN 0-7524-0017-7

Rhondda
Simon Eckley and Emrys Jenkins
ISBN 0-7524-0028-2

Rhondda: A Second Selection
Simon Eckley and Emrys Jenkins
ISBN 0-7524-0308-7

Roath, Splott, and Adamsdown
Roath Local History Society
ISBN 0-7524-0199-8

GLOUCESTERSHIRE

Barnwood, Hucclecote and Brockworth
Alan Sutton
ISBN 0-7524-0000-2

Forest to Severn
Humphrey Phelps
ISBN 0-7524-0008-8

Filton and the Flying Machine
Malcolm Hall
ISBN 0-7524-0171-8

Gloster Aircraft Company
Derek James
ISBN 0-7524-0038-X

The City of Gloucester
Jill Voyce
ISBN 0-7524-0306-0

Around Nailsworth and Minchinhampton from the Conway Collection
Howard Beard
ISBN 0-7524-0048-7

Around Newent
Tim Ward
ISBN 0-7524-0003-7

Stroud: Five Stroud Photographers
Howard Beard, Peter Harris and Wilf Merrett
ISBN 0-7524-0305-2

HAMPSHIRE

Gosport
Ian Edelman
ISBN 0-7524-0300-1

Winchester from the Sollars Collection
John Brimfield
ISBN 0-7524-0173-4

HEREFORDSHIRE

Ross-on-Wye
Tom Rigby and Alan Sutton
ISBN 0-7524-0002-9

HERTFORDSHIRE

Buntingford
Philip Plumb
ISBN 0-7524-0170-X

Hampstead Garden Suburb
Mervyn Miller
ISBN 0-7524-0319-2

Hemel Hempstead
Eve Davis
ISBN 0-7524-0167-X

Letchworth
Mervyn Miller
ISBN 0-7524-0318-4

Welwyn Garden City
Angela Eserin
ISBN 0-7524-0133-5

KENT

Hythe
Joy Melville and Angela Lewis-Johnson
ISBN 0-7524-0169-6

North Thanet Coast
Alan Kay
ISBN 0-7524-0112-2

Shorts Aircraft
Mike Hooks
ISBN 0-7524-0193-9

LANCASHIRE

Lancaster and the Lune Valley
Robert Alston
ISBN 0-7524-0015-0

Morecambe Bay
Robert Alston
ISBN 0-7524-0163-7

Manchester
Peter Stewart
ISBN 0-7524-0103-3

LINCOLNSHIRE

Louth
David Cuppleditch
ISBN 0-7524-0172-6

Stamford
David Gerard
ISBN 0-7524-0309-5

LONDON
(Greater London and Middlesex)

Battersea and Clapham
Patrick Loobey
ISBN 0-7524-0010-X

Canning Town
Howard Bloch and Nick Harris
ISBN 0-7524-0057-6

Chiswick
Carolyn and Peter Hammond
ISBN 0-7524-0001-0

Forest Gate
Nick Harris and Dorcas Sanders
ISBN 0-7524-0049-5

Greenwich
Barbara Ludlow
ISBN 0-7524-0045-2

Highgate and Muswell Hill
Joan Schwitzer and Ken Gay
ISBN 0-7524-0119-X

Islington
Gavin Smith
ISBN 0-7524-0140-8

Lewisham
John Coulter and Barry Olley
ISBN 0-7524-0059-2

Leyton and Leytonstone
Keith Romig and Peter Lawrence
ISBN 0-7524-0158-0

Newham Dockland
Howard Bloch
ISBN 0-7524-0107-6

Norwood
Nicholas Reed
ISBN 0-7524-0147-5

Peckham and Nunhead
John D. Beasley
ISBN 0-7524-0122-X

Piccadilly Circus
David Oxford
ISBN 0-7524-0196-3

Stoke Newington
Gavin Smith
ISBN 0-7524-0159-9

Sydenham and Forest Hill
John Coulter and John Seaman
ISBN 0-7524-0036-3

Wandsworth
Patrick Loobey
ISBN 0-7524-0026-6

Wanstead and Woodford
Ian Dowling and Nick Harris
ISBN 0-7524-0113-0

MONMOUTHSHIRE

Vanished Abergavenny
Frank Olding
ISBN 0-7524-0034-7

Abertillery, Aberbeeg and Llanhilleth
Abertillery and District Museum Society and Simon Eckley
ISBN 0-7524-0134-3

Blaina, Nantyglo and Brynmawr
Trevor Rowson
ISBN 0-7524-0136-X

NORFOLK

North Norfolk
Cliff Richard Temple
ISBN 0-7524-0149-1

NOTTINGHAMSHIRE

Nottingham 1897–1947
Douglas Whitworth
ISBN 0-7524-0157-2

OXFORDSHIRE

Banbury
Tom Rigby
ISBN 0-7524-0013-4

PEMBROKESHIRE

Saundersfoot and Tenby
Ken Daniels
ISBN 0-7524-0192-0

RADNORSHIRE

Llandrindod Wells
Chris Wilson
ISBN 0-7524-0191-2

SHROPSHIRE

Leominster
Eric Turton
ISBN 0-7524-0307-9

Ludlow
David Lloyd
ISBN 0-7524-0155-6

Oswestry
Bernard Mitchell
ISBN 0-7524-0032-0

North Telford: Wellington, Oakengates, and Surrounding Areas
John Powell and Michael A. Vanns
ISBN 0-7524-0124-6

South Telford: Ironbridge Gorge, Madeley, and Dawley
John Powell and Michael A. Vanns
ISBN 0-7524-0125-4

SOMERSET

Bath
Paul De'Ath
ISBN 0-7524-0127-0

Around Yeovil
Robin Ansell and Marion Barnes
ISBN 0-7524-0178-5

STAFFORDSHIRE

Cannock Chase
Sherry Belcher and Mary Mills
ISBN 0-7524-0051-7

Around Cheadle
George Short
ISBN 0-7524-0022-3

The Potteries
Ian Lawley
ISBN 0-7524-0046-0

East Staffordshire
Geoffrey Sowerby and Richard Farman
ISBN 0-7524-0197-1

SUFFOLK

Lowestoft to Southwold
Humphrey Phelps
ISBN 0-7524-0108-4

Walberswick to Felixstowe
Humphrey Phelps
ISBN 0-7524-0109-2

SURREY

Around Camberley
Ken Clarke
ISBN 0-7524-0148-3

Around Cranleigh
Michael Miller
ISBN 0-7524-0143-2

Epsom and Ewell
Richard Essen
ISBN 0-7524-0111-4

Farnham by the Wey
Jean Parratt
ISBN 0-7524-0185-8

Industrious Surrey: Historic Images of the County at Work
Chris Shepheard
ISBN 0-7524-0009-6

Reigate and Redhill
Mary G. Goss
ISBN 0-7524-0179-3

Richmond and Kew
Richard Essen
ISBN 0-7524-0145-9

SUSSEX

Billingshurst
Wendy Lines
ISBN 0-7524-0301-X

WARWICKSHIRE

Central Birmingham 1870–1920
Keith Turner
ISBN 0-7524-0053-3

Old Harborne
Roy Clarke
ISBN 0-7524-0054-1

WILTSHIRE

Malmesbury
Dorothy Barnes
ISBN 0-7524-0177-7

Great Western Swindon
Tim Bryan
ISBN 0-7524-0153-X

Midland and South Western Junction Railway
Mike Barnsley and Brian Bridgeman
ISBN 0-7524-0016-9

WORCESTERSHIRE

Around Malvern
Keith Smith
ISBN 0-7524-0029-0

YORKSHIRE
(EAST RIDING)

Hornsea
G.L. Southwell
ISBN 0-7524-0120-3

YORKSHIRE
(NORTH RIDING)

Northallerton
Vera Chapman
ISBN 0-7524-055-X

Scarborough in the 1970s and 1980s
Richard Percy
ISBN 0-7524-0325-7

YORKSHIRE
(WEST RIDING)

Barnsley
Barnsley Archive Service
ISBN 0-7524-0188-2

Bingley
Bingley and District Local History Society
ISBN 0-7524-0311-7

Bradford
Gary Firth
ISBN 0-7524-0313-3

Castleford
Wakefield Metropolitan District Council
ISBN 0-7524-0047-9

Doncaster
Peter Tuffrey
ISBN 0-7524-0162-9

Harrogate
Malcolm Neesam
ISBN 0-7524-0154-8

Holme Valley
Peter and Iris Bullock
ISBN 0-7524-0139-4

Horsforth
Alan Cockroft and Matthew Young
ISBN 0-7524-0130-0

Knaresborough
Arnold Kellett
ISBN 0-7524-0131-9

Around Leeds
Matthew Young and Dorothy Payne
ISBN 0-7524-0168-8

Penistone
Matthew Young and David Hambleton
ISBN 0-7524-0138-6

Selby from the William Rawling Collection
Matthew Young
ISBN 0-7524-0198-X

Central Sheffield
Martin Olive
ISBN 0-7524-0011-8

Around Stocksbridge
Stocksbridge and District History Society
ISBN 0-7524-0165-3

TRANSPORT

Filton and the Flying Machine
Malcolm Hall
ISBN 0-7524-0171-8

Gloster Aircraft Company
Derek James
ISBN 0-7524-0038-X

Great Western Swindon
Tim Bryan
ISBN 0-7524-0153-X

Midland and South Western Junction Railway
Mike Barnsley and Brian Bridgeman
ISBN 0-7524-0016-9

Shorts Aircraft
Mike Hooks
ISBN 0-7524-0193-9

This stock list shows all titles available in the United Kingdom as at 30 September 1995.

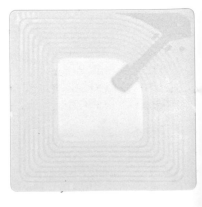

ORDER FORM

The books in this stock list are available from your local bookshop. Alternatively they are available by mail order at a totally inclusive price of £10.00 per copy.

For overseas orders please add the following postage supplement for each copy ordered:
> European Union £0.36 (this includes the Republic of Ireland)
> Royal Mail Zone 1 (for example, U.S.A. and Canada) £1.96
> Royal Mail Zone 2 (for example, Australia and New Zealand) £2.47

Please note that all of these supplements are actual Royal Mail charges with no profit element to the Chalford Publishing Company. Furthermore, as the Air Mail Printed Papers rate applies, we are restricted from enclosing any personal correspondence other than to indicate the senders name

Payment can be made by cheque, Visa or Mastercard. Please indicate your method of payment on this order form.

If you are not entirely happy with your purchase you may return it within 30 days of receipt for a full refund.

Please send your order to:

> The Chalford Publishing Company,
> St Mary's Mill,
> Chalford,
> Stroud,
> Gloucestershire
> GL6 8NX

This order form should perforate away from the book. However, if you are reluctant to damage the book in any way we are quite happy to accept a photocopy order form or a letter containing the necessary information.

PLEASE WRITE CLEARLY USING BLOCK CAPITALS

Name and address of the person ordering the books listed below:

_____

_____

_____ Post code _____

Please also supply your telephone number in case we have difficulty fully understanding your requirements.   Tel.: _____ - _____

Name and address of where the books are to be despatched to (if different from above):

_____

_____

_____ Post code _____

Please indicate here if you would like to receive future information on books published by the Chalford Publishing Company.

____ Yes, please put me on your mailing list   ____ No, please just send the books ordered below

Title	ISBN	Quantity
....	0-7524-_____-___	_____
....	0-7524-_____-___	_____
....	0-7524-_____-___	_____
....	0-7524-_____-___	_____
....	0-7524-_____-___	_____
	Total number of books	_____

Cost of books delivered in UK = Number of books ordered @ £10 each =£ _____

Overseas postage supplement (if relevant)   =£ _____

TOTAL PAYMENT   =£ _____

Method of Payment   ❏ Cheque   ❏ Visa   ❏ Mastercard   **VISA**

Please make cheques payable to *The Chalford Publishing Company*   MasterCard

Name of Card Holder   _____

Card Number ❏❏❏❏❏❏❏❏❏❏❏❏❏❏❏❏❏❏❏

Expiry date ❏❏ / ❏❏

I authorise payment of £_____ from the above card

Signed _____